Human Resources
Business Process
Outsourcing

Edward E. Lawler III
Dave Ulrich
Jac Fitz-enz
James C. Madden V

With Regina Maruca

Human Resources Business Process Outsourcing

Transforming How HR Gets Its Work Done

JOSSEY-BASS
A Wiley Imprint
www.josseybass.com

Published by Jossey-Bass
A Wiley Imprint
989 Market Street, San Francisco, CA 94103-1741   www.josseybass.com

Jossey-Bass books and products are available through most bookstores. To contact Jossey-Bass directly call our Customer Care Department within the U.S. at 800-956-7739, outside the U.S. at 317-572-3986 or fax 317-572-4002.

Jossey-Bass also publishes its books in a variety of electronic formats. Some content that appears in print may not be available in electronic books.

Library of Congress Cataloging-in-Publication Data

Human resources business process outsourcing : transforming how HR gets its work done / by Edward E. Lawler III ... [et al.].—1st ed.
   p. cm.—(The Jossey-Bass business & management series)
  "A Wiley Imprint."
  Includes bibliographical references and index.
 ISBN 0-7879-7163-4 (alk. paper)
  1. Personnel management—Contracting out. I. Lawler, Edward E. II. Series.
  HF5549.H865 2004
  658.3—dc22   2004011139

Printed in the United States of America
FIRST EDITION
HB Printing 10 9 8 7 6 5 4 3 2 1

The Jossey-Bass

Business & Management Series

Contents

Preface

Above all else, this book is about how the role of the human resources (HR) function can be redefined in order to create more effective organizations. Major changes in business conditions have placed new and increased demands on the HR function. To meet these demands, some of the traditional HR work must be done differently, and HR needs to provide new services. HR must excel at both delivering traditional transaction services and providing high value-added strategic services. If HR stays at the transactional level, the department will become an afterthought. If HR goes strategic but lacks the ability to deliver on operational tasks, it will lose credibility.

Finding new and innovative ways to do HR-related transactional (administrative) work should be a concern for both business leaders and HR professionals. The same is true for finding ways HR can contribute to the formation and implementation of business plans and strategies. Business leaders need to raise the bar for the function by stating what is expected from HR professionals. HR professionals need to change their views about what HR can and should deliver and how HR should be organized. We believe that the HR function can help leaders build competitive organizations and that HR organizations can be organized so that they create value, not just costs. In order for this to happen, HR professionals must redefine their role and acquire new competencies.

Business leaders and HR professionals are both targets of this work. When business leaders understand the untapped potential within the HR function, we believe they will raise their expectations. When HR professionals understand the new realities they face and the new ways of delivering value that are available to them, we believe it will make a difference in how they work and in what they accomplish.

Our target audience includes all managers because when they find that HR activities can help them deliver value, they are supportive of a new, high-value-added role for HR. We want to ensure that line managers understand what HR can do and to encourage them to demand high value from HR professionals who are competent and committed to delivering that value.

One reality HR faces is that it cannot abandon its transactional work in favor of developing strategic expertise. If the function "goes strategic" and lacks the ability to deliver on its operational responsibilities, it will become irrelevant as quickly as if it had stayed focused on only administrative tasks. But there is a middle ground— a new territory for HR that presents a provocative opportunity for professionals in the field: creating an HR function that excels at both the delivery of traditional transaction services and high-value-added strategic services.

And so it is left to HR departments the world over to decide how, how much, and how quickly they want to change. We have written this book to explore the new territory; it is about how leaders can redefine HR roles and operations in order to create more effective organizations. It is full of valuable information about how the HR function can dramatically increase the value it adds to corporations, whether they adopt an HR outsourcing model or not. The book also should provide anyone who is considering adopting the HR BPO approach with invaluable information about the issues they need to consider and the potential advantages of doing HR BPO.

We think of the HR function as having a "demand" side and a "supply" side. Our first chapter focuses on the demand side, aspiring to answer the question, What are the new demands business leaders must meet in order to succeed? More specifically, Chapter One explores the new realities of business from the point of view of senior executives charged with creating a company that will compete and win, and then it spells out how these business realities create increased demand for HR services and actions.

Chapter Two focuses on the "supply" side of the equation. In it, we seek to answer the questions: What can HR departments do to deliver value? What new business models for delivering HR will work? How can HR contribute to organizational effectiveness?

The answers to these questions raise an additional query: How does one measure the effectiveness of HR? This is the focus of Chapter Three. Our sense is that for any successful, sustainable change to occur in the services and output of the HR function, managers must first have a grounding in where they currently stand in terms of value delivered, value added, and cost to serve. Chapter Three offers a template for that analysis.

In Chapter Four, we turn to the exploration of how the HR function in corporations is structured. Our aim here is to explain the new approaches that organizations are taking, identify what options they have, and spell out how they should organize their HR function in the future.

We have had the unique opportunity to study Exult, an HR business process outsourcer (BPO), from its early days in 1999 to the announcement of its merger with Hewitt Associates in June 2004. We have had in-depth access to the company's top management team and customers. Chapter Five begins our exploration of the HR BPO approach in action with a case study of Exult. We offer it for two reasons. First, we think the story of an entrepreneurial start-up in this field provides a view of how an important HR market space has evolved in its early years. Our aim is to provide an understanding of how a major provider in the industry thinks of its business model and how that model is evolving as the field matures.

Second, and quite aside from the particulars of the Exult case, we think that an inside look at any successful start-up in these turbulent times offers lessons to managers who are poised on the brink of a significant change effort. Transforming HR is about more than cost control and taking a twenty-first-century approach to administrative paperwork; it is also about developing a compelling business case for a function that hopes to add new value to its organization. In that sense, HR departments the world over are potential "start-ups."

We have also had the opportunity to examine, in depth, four early-mover companies that contracted with Exult for a range of HR BPO services as part of the process of transforming their HR departments. Chapters Six through Nine offer case studies on the process of transforming HR at British Petroleum, Bank of America, International Paper, and Prudential. We hope that these cases will help readers understand the creation and evolution of the HR BPO industry and help them understand what is involved in HR BPO so that they can make an informed decision about whether it is right for their organization.

In Chapter Ten, we turn to summary thoughts and offer the results of a survey and interviews we conducted in order to create a report card of sorts on our four cases' efforts to reinvent their HR functions. It is not surprising that in every aspect of transforming their HR functions, the companies had both substantive successes and significant setbacks. We think their experiences contain transferable lessons that can help readers learn from the efforts of those who have gone before them. Finally, in the last chapter, we look ahead and identify the key issues that will affect the long-term development and effectiveness of HR BPO.

We need to make several points about the roles that the authors took in writing this book. Ed Lawler took overall responsibility for the fine-tuning and the integration of the book; he also contributed to each of the chapters. Dave Ulrich took major responsibility for Chapters One and Two, while Jac Fitz-enz took responsibility for Chapter Three. Because of his role as CEO of Exult, James Madden took major responsibility for Chapter Five on Exult. He also provided coordination and access with respect to the four Exult case studies.

The writing of the case studies was done by Regina Maruca, a professional writer. Content responsibility for these chapters remained in the hands of Ed Lawler. This is a critical point with respect to the writing because of the potential conflict of interest Jim Madden, as president and CEO of Exult, has with respect to the way these case studies are presented. In order to maintain the integrity of the case studies, as well as the integrity of the two concluding chapters, responsibility for these rested with the "non-Exult" authors.

We want to thank the many people who have contributed to the writing of this book. Many of the employees of the four case study companies gave freely of their time for interviews, as did a number of Exult employees. Kevin Campbell, the chief operating officer of Exult, deserves special thanks. He provided data about Exult as well as access to the four case study companies. Special thanks also go to Regina Maruca for her work on the case studies and on the overall editing of the book.

May 2004

Edward E. Lawler III
Los Angeles, California

Dave Ulrich
Ann Arbor, Michigan

Jac Fitz-enz
Santa Clara, California

James C. Madden V
Irvine, California

The Authors

Edward E. Lawler III is Distinguished Professor of Business and director of the Center for Effective Organizations (CEO) at the Marshall School of Business, University of Southern California (USC). He joined USC in 1978 and during 1979 founded and became director of CEO. He has consulted with over one hundred organizations on employee involvement, organizational change, and compensation and has been honored as a top contributor to the fields of human resources management, organizational development, organizational behavior, and compensation. The author of over three hundred articles and thirty-five books, his articles have appeared in leading academic journals, as well as *Fortune, Harvard Business Review,* and leading newspapers. His most recent books include *Rewarding Excellence* (Jossey-Bass, 2000), *Corporate Boards: New Strategies for Adding Value at the Top* (Jossey-Bass, 2001), *Organizing for High Performance* (Jossey-Bass, 2001), *Treat People Right* (Jossey-Bass, 2003), and *Creating a Strategic Human Resources Organization* (Stanford University Press, 2003).

Dave Ulrich is professor of business at the University of Michigan. He studies how organizations build capabilities of speed, learning, collaboration, accountability, talent, and leadership through leveraging human resources. *BusinessWeek* named him the number 1 management educator in 2001, and he has won numerous other distinctions and awards. He has published over one hundred articles and book chapters and is author or coauthor of twelve books, including *Why the Bottom Line Isn't* (Wiley, 2003), *The GE-Workout*

(McGraw-Hill, 2002), *The HR Scorecard* (Harvard University Press, 2001), *Results Based Leadership* (Harvard University Press, 1999), *Human Resource Champions* (Harvard University Press, 1997), and *The Boundaryless Organization* (Jossey-Bass, 1995). He was the editor of *Human Resource Management Journal*, has served on the editorial board of four other journals, is on the board of directors for Herman Miller, is a fellow in the National Academy of Human Resources, and cofounded the Michigan Human Resource Partnership. He has consulted and done research with over half of the Fortune 200 companies. Currently he is on sabbatical as president of the Canada Montreal Mission for the Church of Jesus Christ of Latter-Day Saints.

Jac Fitz-enz, chief executive officer of Human Capital Resource, is acknowledged as the father of human capital strategy and benchmarking. As the founder and chairman of Saratoga Institute, he led the development of the world's most comprehensive human capital benchmark database. These metrics have been endorsed as the standard for the human resources profession by the Society for Human Resources Management (SHRM). He has published over 160 articles, reports, and book chapters covering human capital valuation, leadership, human resources strategy and benchmarking, talent attraction and retention, employee productivity, performance measurement, and outsourcing. He is the author of seven books on human capital and organizational management and is the only two-time recipient of the SHRM Book of the Year Award, for *Human Value Management* (Jossey-Bass, 1990) and *The ROI of Human Capital* (Amacom, 2000). He has trained more than sixty thousand managers in forty countries and was named Superstar HR Outsourcing Specialist by *HR Outsourcing Today* in 2003. He serves on advisory councils for PeopleSoft, PricewaterhouseCooper's Saratoga Institute, Exult, CRI, and Brassring.

James C. Madden V is founder, chairman, and chief executive officer of Exult, the innovator and market leader in human resources business process outsourcing for Global 500 corporations. He has been a pioneer in the human resources outsourcing industry and has served in outsourcing leadership positions at Systemhouse, Booz-Allen & Hamilton, and Andersen Consulting (now Accenture). In 2002, Madden received the PricewaterhouseCoopers/Michael F. Corbett & Associates Outsourcing World Achievement Award and the *Orange County Business Journal*/Ernst & Young Excellence in Entrepreneurship Award. Madden devotes time to a number of civic, community, and business organizations, including the Hoag Hospital Foundation and TechNet, a technology industry advocacy group.

Regina Fazio Maruca is a ghostwriter, editor, and writing coach who specializes in leadership, management, and marketing topics. A former senior editor at the *Harvard Business Review*, her own byline has appeared in publications including *HBR* and *Fast Company*.

Human Resources
Business Process
Outsourcing

Chapter One

Forces for Change

Human resources (HR) departments are at an important crossroads. Large-scale transformation of the HR function is not only desirable; it is necessary. Why? First, the traditional transactional work of HR is rapidly becoming a commodity; at many companies, there are significant cost savings to be realized by treating it in this manner. Top managers are increasingly aware of the efficiencies that new technologies can provide, and they are putting pressure on the HR function to reduce costs as never before. Second, there is a growing demand for expertise regarding the deployment and management of human capital and organizational capability; the HR function can and should provide that expertise.[1] Managers at all levels increasingly need strategic guidance about how they deploy their workforce and build their organizations in order to fulfill company goals.

In order to respond effectively to both pressures, the HR function must simultaneously create transaction efficiencies and transformational changes. But substantive change in the nature of a staff function's work and role is rare. What's more, when such change does occur, it is usually driven by forces outside the department, such as a merger, a divestiture, a technology change, a change in the economy, or a new business strategy. Rarely do staff functions step up to reinvent themselves.

Currently, most HR leaders can still choose whether they will respond to change or whether they will lead change. HR executives still have the opportunity to shape how they and the HR function respond to the demands that their function is experiencing. To us, the path is clear. We believe that HR executives who stick with the status quo and maintain a focus on transactional work will soon become obsolete. At the same time, we believe that HR professionals who meet the need for strategic expertise concerning human capital management and organizational effectiveness will contribute value that far exceeds the past contributions of the HR function. In the process, they will make themselves indispensable to their organizations.

A Case of Supply and Demand

To assess the nature and extent of the change required of HR, imagine a simple demand-supply model for businesses and apply that model to the future of HR. Start by stepping back and considering the major factors that are placing new or shifting demands on businesses today.[2] Since top managers grapple with these issues, HR professionals need to understand and respond to them in order to add value and establish their worth:

- *Customer-firm interactions are evolving.* Customers have more access to information and are more informed than ever before. As a result, customer expectations are higher than ever before, and competition for customer share is greater than ever before. Customers expect—and usually get—lower cost and higher-quality goods and services; as a result, they put pressure on organizations to reduce their own costs even as they strive to improve quality.[3]

HR directly affects operating costs because of the cost of its own operation and because it is partially responsible for a major expense: wages and benefits. In addition, the quality of HR services influences product and service costs and quality because the quality of HR services affects employee behavior and performance.

- *Targeting key customers is increasingly important.* At eBay, 10 percent of the customers purchase 90 percent of the products; in the airline industry, 10 percent of the customers provide 40 percent of revenue and 60 percent of profit. Financial service firms strive for share of wallet; food product firms seek share of stomach. In each of these cases, new customer realities have established new rules for winning; customer share is now more important in these scenarios than market share.

To gain a critical customer share, companies must build a value proposition uniquely tailored to a particular target customer. Amazon, for example, knows the book buying patterns of those who buy more books and can tailor its offerings to those target customers. General Motors knows the car buying patterns of those who replace cars more frequently with new cars than others and can tailor its offerings to those customers.

Companies must also shift their focus from winning a single customer transaction to winning a lifetime of transactions. Amazon wants not only to sell a book, but also to build a relationship with customers so that they will spend a high portion of their lifetime book buying money with Amazon. As a result, Amazon needs to build a customer share strategy, directed at target customers, through brand loyalty and the kind of exceptional service that can be delivered only by a skilled, committed workforce.

One way to increase customer intimacy in key customer groups is to involve these customers in significant company activities that are designed to improve service levels. By involving customers in HR activities (for example, by participating in the design and delivery of training activities), HR practices may be used to create intimacy with targeted customers. When leaders worry about employees as if they are customers and customers as if they are employees, both customers and employees are more engaged and committed. When HR practices are used to align both employees and customers, both employee and customer share grows.

- *Information technology is continuing to evolve.* As we all know, information is increasingly ubiquitous and also increasingly easier to access and manipulate. This trend has significant implications for business-to-business, business-to-supplier, and business-to-employee relationships.[4] It is also the foundation of e-business operations. Information technology allows for warehousing the kinds of customer data that enable companies to identify specific customers and determine their buying criteria. Such data also allow customers to be targeted for life, as companies continually update their knowledge of customers' behaviors and buying criteria.

Information about employees allows companies to personalize employee rewards and better understand their employees' expertise, potential to contribute value, and likely career paths. Information warehouses can make it possible for organizations to analyze employee data to determine the costs and effectiveness of their HR practices and the degree to which they support key business strategies.

Information, in other words, increasingly is both a revenue source and a source of competitive advantage. Computer access companies like Time Warner and Yahoo increasingly make money on the information they track on their users. Firms with better information about customers, for example, can make decisions to move into new markets more quickly than their competition. Unilever tracks consumer buying patterns based on a number of demographic inputs such as household income, marital status, size of household, and household gender makeup. Using this information, Unilever targets its marketing not only to a region or geography, but also to a particular household through coupons and advertising. Consumer information becomes a source of competitive advantage because Unilever knows better than its competitors what consumers want and expect.

Similarly, firms with enhanced understanding of their employees' strengths and weaknesses are better able to make strategic decisions that will stick and succeed. A company that understands at the outset whether it has the capabilities to expand into a new market and where it needs to bolster its capabilities has a competitive advantage over companies that do not know themselves as well.

The implications of the growing importance of information for HR are obvious: HR must continue updating its systems and provide current and accurate data on employees, HR practices, and organizational outcomes. HR must also help turn information into informed choices so that data are not just warehoused but used to improve decision making.[5] HR must help business leaders generate and use information to help their organizations compete. HR systems must support change, using technology faster and deploying it more routinely.[6]

HR practices also need to adjust to the increasing availability of information technology. Staffing with information technology (such as computer databases and Internet screening of candidates) allows employers to identify and screen a broader array of candidates. Development with information technology (IT) allows for remote learning. Compensation management with technology allows for decisions to be made rapidly and accurately. IT-based self-service, when it comes to HR administration, can reduce the cost of HR as well as provide faster service.

• *Mergers, acquisitions, divestures, alliances, and partnerships are changing the shape of industry at a rapid rate.* Mergers and acquisitions continue to occur, and in some significant cases, they have crossed traditional industry boundaries to create convergence across boundaries.[7] For example, the merger and alliance activity in the airline industry has redefined the industry. Today, convergence means that airlines sometimes compete with organizations outside their industry. For example, frequent flier programs are key assets to the airlines, but now these companies play in the same competitive arena as retail stores, telephone companies, and restaurants in deploying frequent flier benefits. Similarly, financial service firms worry about customers banking through Internet firms, about supermarkets performing financial services, and about traditional manufacturing firms like General Motors and General Electric performing financing functions.

Industry consolidation also means that products that were once in the purview of only one industry now cross boundaries. Computer monitors may become televisions and vice versa; telephones are now cameras. Vehicle on-line services like General Motors's On-Star make the automotive company a player in communication services; utility firms now offer control services to manage home and commercial temperature; and the electronics inside appliances now allow washing machines, refrigerators, and the like to be directly connected to central services for maintenance and monitoring usage.

As industries evolve in this manner, leaders seek creative and alternative ways to leverage their organizations' core competencies and organizational capabilities across industry boundaries. At the heart of both are people. HR systems that help people conceive innovative ways to define and navigate industry boundaries can become an important competitive edge.

- *Investors are changing their assessments of value.* Determining a firm's market value has always been important to investors and managers alike. Recent research on market value has shown that the tangible financial assets of a firm predict less of its total market value today than in the past.[8] A firm's total market value thus increasingly comes from the intangible assets that a firm possesses.

In exploring intangibles, investors look behind the financial numbers to determine the market value of a firm. They examine intangibles that predict future results, and this affects the current market value of corporations. Intangibles such as quality of leadership, speed of response, ability to innovate, capacity to integrate acquisitions, accountability for results, culture, and talent are becoming a central part of a firm's total shareholder value proposition.

Leaders have the primary responsibility for creating sustainable intangible value, but HR professionals can help in shaping intangibles. The goal is to build organizations whose long-term viability is ensured by the way the organization operates internally. HR professionals can contribute by developing HR systems that are designed to attract, deploy, motivate, and engage human capital in ways that create superior intangibles.

Consider that the ethics and values of senior management are among the most critical intangibles. When senior leaders are seen as greedy and excessively self-interested, investors discount the market value of the firm's financial performance. When leaders are forthcoming with problems and honest in assessments—that is, when they operate ethically—investors award firms positive intangible value.

Ethics and integrity have become a social agenda that leaders must explicitly acknowledge and manage.[9] This agenda has a number of dimensions. For example, it encompasses legal issues. When leaders violate the laws that govern organizations and society, either explicitly through their actions or implicitly by turning away from and ignoring others' behavior, they fall into an ethics black hole that results in lost credibility. Customers, investors, and employees lose faith.

Leaders who assume large and visible organizational roles must live to a high standard, their behavior beyond reproach. Even the appearance of misdoing often leads to an erosion of confidence from critical stakeholders. Leaders, because of their status, economic rewards, and opportunities to influence, must be cautious about their behavior and the ways in which others view that behavior.

One important way that organizations shape social values is through their HR practices. For example, rewards often communicate a social value. When the only performance metric is financial returns (such as cash flow), pay for performance becomes a way of signaling what the organization values. If performance includes a more balanced scorecard, then leaders will change their behavior to reflect what is measured.[10]

Leaders need confidants who advise them on social issues and offer candid counsel and feedback on their behavior and on how to make informed social choices. HR professionals can be a voice for creating a social agenda and a source of candid feedback on ethical issues.

• *Social trends are affecting product, customer, and employee expectations*. Many social trends affect how leaders and organizations act.[11] The recent heightened emphasis on exemplary leadership behavior is one. The widening gap between the haves and have-nots is another. This bifurcation of the population has become more acute with the development of technology. The haves have access to computers and the Web, which leverages their knowledge and breadth of influence. The have-nots have little access to technology, which limits their scope of influence and thinking.

Business leaders often experience primarily the haves in their day-to-day work and may not be sensitive to the have-nots. Sometimes leaders live in "affluence ghettos," whereby they work with people who are educated, successful, and ambitious; they live in the same neighborhoods as these people; their children attend the same schools; they socialize in the same areas; and they shop in the same stores. An affluence ghetto constrains a leader's perception of the range of people who might work for or buy from his or her organization and in doing so limits the organization's potential to grow.

Leaders need to be sensitive to the reality that their background is not always the background of those who buy the company's products or of employees who make and sell those products. For the benefit of their organizations, they need to seek talented employees from multiple sources and leverage diverse backgrounds into common approaches.

• *Globalization is increasingly affecting organizations.* One of this book's authors often asks this question in a workshop he conducts for alternating groups of about one hundred people: "What countries have you received e-mails from in the last week or so?" Generally, the count gets to twenty-five or thirty. This simple exercise reflects the increasingly global economy. When information moves across boundaries in "computer time" and when ideas from one country transfer easily to another, we clearly live in a global village. The realities of globalization, with information, ideas, jobs, and people moving readily around the world, create complex leadership challenges.

It is well known that leaders must learn to create global organizations that can both leverage global scale and adapt locally, move information quickly from one site to another, manage the diversity of cultures while maintaining unity of focus, and manage employees in dispersed operations around the globe.[12] It is much less understood that HR issues are often central to global success. Yet knowing how to attract, motivate, and retain talent in one region of the world does not necessarily mean knowing how to do the same in another region. Reward systems may also vary. Being global in business requires being global in organizational design, people, and HR practices.

The new business realities we have reviewed are summarized in Table 1.1. Taken together, they constitute the tremendous amount of change that organizations face today. These changes represent a potential threat to the HR function if it fails to respond to them. But they also represent a profound opportunity for HR to take on a new, more important role because so many of the new imperatives in business are directly related to the expertise and services that the HR profession can offer.

The Supply Side of the Equation

In responding to the demands they face, organizations and their leaders need to do more than craft strategy. Competitiveness requires both strategy and organization. Merely drafting a strategy that declares a new vision is necessary but not sufficient to win. Winning also requires creating an organization that accomplishes stated goals. Organization is more than structure; it is the set of capabilities a firm possesses. Capabilities represent what the firm is able to do well, its culture, and its unique identity. These capabilities derive from an integrated set of HR investments, where HR practices of staffing, training, rewards, communication, organizational design, workplace design, and so forth are aligned around building capability.[13]

The reality of the competitive business environment is that organizations can be successful only when they focus on doing those activities that help accomplish strategic objectives through core competencies and organizational capabilities. If organizations lack all the core competencies and organizational capabilities they need to succeed, they must build relationships with partners who can fill the gaps. The implications of this point are profound: filling gaps in vital capabilities can lead organizations to outsource any number of functions, from manufacturing to staff services such as IT and HR management. The key is ensuring that each partner supplies clear value so that the whole, which can be seen in the value delivered to customers, reduced costs, and ensuing profits, is greater than the sum of its parts.

Table 1.1 Challenges Facing Organizations

Area	Issues	General Manager Questions	Human Resource Questions
Customer	Cost/quality: Customer expects continuous improvement in quality and cost share of customer versus market share—for example, Coke wants "share of stomach" versus market share	How do I target key customers and develop intimacy with them? How do I measure share of customer?	How do we reduce the cost of HR services and improve quality? How do we use HR practices to build relationships with targeted customers?
	Disintermediation: New channels to go to customers—for example, Amazon sells book over the Web		
	Information: More informed customers—for example, consumers go on-line to study health options		
	Brand: Building firm equity—for example, some firms (Coke, Intel, Nike) have powerful brands		
	Consumer: More informed (literacy), disposable income, more sophisticated with choice, demanding—for example, buyer power		
Information technology	Digitalization: Rapid change in technology and information access (miniaturization)—for example, telephones, TV, washing machines	How do I make information technology investments that will create value?	How do we get the right people and processes to ensure information technology advances?
	e-business: New channels, customer intimacy, Web strategy		

Table 1.1 Challenges Facing Organizations, Cont'd.

Area	Issues	General Manager Questions	Human Resource Questions
Investors	Value: Defining value as shareholder return, not cash Intangibles: Importance of intangibles and how to identify, measure, track—for example, market value Diversification of capital markets: 1979 = 524 mutual funds; 1999 = 7,791	How do I identify, build, and communicate intangibles?	How do we create intangible value through HR practices?
Business structures	Mergers: Consolidation, alliances, partnerships Divestiture: Break-up of firms, start-up firms, niche players, new players (for example, Jet Blue)	How do I position my organization within a changing business landscape?	How do we adjust HR practices to core competency needs?
Social	Haves versus have-nots: Widening gap of those who have and those who do not—a global issue Economic uncertainty: Dealing with ambiguity about the future and rapid pace of change	What social responsibility do I have?	How do we modify HR practices to deal with different employee needs?
Global	Virtual organization: Networked, dispersed organization Global leverage: Learning to leverage global enterprise with local autonomy Managing at a distance: Keeping common identity	What are the global implications for my business?	How do we adapt HR practices to global conditions?

Table 1.1 Challenges Facing Organizations, Cont'd.

Area	Issues	General Manager Questions	Human Resource Questions
Organization	New organization structures: Flatter, horizontal, shared services	How do I build an organization that helps me win?	How do we modify HR practices to new organizational forms to build competencies and capabilities?
	Employee expectations: Next-generation employees, free agent employees (low loyalty), work-life balance issues, desire for challenging work		
Leadership	Leadership: Relying less on authority, need for better leaders	How do we lead effectively in today's competitive environment?	Do our HR practices attract, retain, and develop effective leaders?

Organizational forms are changing. The traditional hierarchy governed by rules, roles, and responsibilities is often not the best way to manage. Instead of rules that govern how employees behave, more and more employees do what they do because of unity of interests. Management by mind-set, or common goals or values, often needs to replace management by objectives. Employees need to focus on getting the work done regardless of formal roles, and managers need to encourage and facilitate such independent and responsible behavior. Because of these changes, new organizational forms (which go by many names, including *horizontal, alliances, networks, boundaryless, lateral structure, lateral,* and *shared services*) need to be used.[14] Leaders need to allocate critical tasks to individuals rather than relying on an organizational chart. Instead of responsibilities laid out in job descriptions and profiles, employees need to join and work in task forces to define and deliver work.

Because of the importance of organization as a source of competitive advantage, companies need expertise in organizational effectiveness. They need to develop new designs and determine how to develop the competencies and capabilities they require in order to implement their strategies. HR can play an important role both in developing strategies that are based on competencies and capabilities and helping organizations and their leaders develop the right competencies and capabilities.

Success in today's business environment requires leaders who are not only aware of but also sensitive to the many changes and demands that organizations face. Managers need to learn to influence less through formal position and more through relationships. If leaders fail to respond to these increasing demands, they will be replaced by executives who do.

The well-chronicled, increasing rate of CEO failure often can be traced to their inability to respond to one or more of the new demands. Sometimes failed CEOs were unable to anticipate technology or customer change, sometimes their actions violated social and legal norms, and sometimes they failed to engage their employees in the process of change. The need for effective managers and leaders at all levels is being felt by virtually every organization. HR is clearly well positioned to help organizations meet this need, and its future undoubtedly will be significantly influenced by how effectively it helps organizations meet it.

HR's Optimal Response

We have mentioned in brief the ways in which HR professionals and the HR function at large can help organizations meet the new demands of doing business. We now consider in greater detail the opportunities HR professionals have to create value for employees, customers, investors, and their organization.

Value for Employees

Many employees want opportunities to learn and to grow. HR professionals need to build a new employee value proposition that both increases and clarifies what employees should give to their organization and what organizations should give to their employees.[15] The new business realities require employees who are able to contribute more productivity, knowledge, and skill than ever before. And when employees make these contributions, they must get more back from the firm. As employee demographics shift, what employees get back may be more focused on accomplishment and development. Employees may get opportunities to learn and grow, a chance to work for an organization with a significant purpose or meaning, a team of peers who share values and offer a cohesive community, access to information about where the organization is headed and why, and flexible policies and practices that adapt to each employee's personal life.

HR professionals can play a major role in crafting HR practices and employee policies that simultaneously articulate what employees are expected to contribute and to receive. HR practices should also be customized to support the business strategy of the organization. Finally, HR can help make a workplace more employee-friendly by offering high-quality user-friendly administrative services.

Value for Customers

In the new business realities, customer share often becomes the dominant criterion.[16] Customer share represents the percentage of total volume a customer does that is garnered by one firm over the lifetime of the customer. Customer share requires that leaders identity target customers—those customers who have both scale (because of their volume of purchases) and opportunity (because of their potential for growth). Once leaders identify target customers, they are able to work to gain share of those customers.

Gaining customer share with targeted customers comes when leaders know how to build more intimate connections with customers. Some connection may come from involving customers in strategic and product decisions by using focus groups, market research, or strategic planning. It may come by using technology to directly link to customers. eBay tracks the buying patterns of its frequent customers (time of day, time of month, type of good purchased, and other parameters) to target key customers. Customer connection may also come from including customers in HR practices of staffing, training, compensation, and organizational design. Target customers can participate in staffing by recommending or screening candidates, in training by delivering or attending the training activity, in compensation by evaluating performance, and in organizational design by participating in task forces.

HR contributes to customer share when HR practices are explicitly linked to meeting the requirements of target customers and when target customers actually participate in defining those HR practices. For example, one hotel chain uses a group of customers in defining the competencies required of its hotel management. These frequent guests of the hotel could articulate what they as target customers wanted to experience in their travels. By working with these customers, the HR practices for hiring, training, and rewarding were defined according to customer requirements.

This hotel chain, in fact, often includes customer input when implementing HR practices. Customers are among those who interview candidates for key positions. They present a portion of an orientation or training seminar. They offer data about their experiences that become part of the appraisal process. The goal of these activities is that the hotel chain will have actions aligned with target customer expectations so that target customers will consistently select this hotel.

To meet the customer share demand and focus HR practices on customers, HR professionals must look beyond HR administration and become much more customer sensitive. They need to know who the target customers are, why they chose one vendor over another, and how existing HR practices can be tweaked to serve customers better.

Value for Investors

Investors increasingly are looking beyond and behind the financial numbers to intangibles, which may range from more visible issues such as brand and research and development investment to organizational capability issues such as quality of leadership. With intangible assets, leaders may create a "story line" for investors that increases credibility and confidence. As a result of this confidence, market value goes up. For example, Herman Miller has more than double the market capitalization than Steelcase, a firm about twice its size, because Herman Miller has known organizational capabilities that give it a higher intangible value in the eyes of investors.

Intangible value comes when investors know about and have confidence that the infrastructure of the firm is able to ensure future earnings. Many of the intangibles investors value come from HR practices. When a firm has a reputation for better talent, faster time to market, more innovative products and services, better collaboration, more ability to learn and share information, and accountability for results, investors value the firm more highly. HR professionals face the demand of performing so that their work adds to the intangible value of their organization.

In order for HR professionals to meet investor demands, they must become knowledgeable about who the firm's investors are, what investor expectations are, and how to communicate to investors the intangibles that matter most. HR professionals may also provide intellectual leadership in performing intangible audits where the intangibles are identified and evaluated and plans made for improvement.

Finally, HR costs are part of the total expenses of doing business. Controlling and getting a good return on investments in training and other HR programs can contribute to the bottom line of a corporation.

Value for Organizations

Some leaders have taken a balanced scorecard approach to measuring organizational effectiveness by focusing on employees, customers, and investors.[17] They believe they can "succeed" by focusing on these three stakeholders. However, we do not think so. The organization is a critical, separate, and independent stakeholder. It has a culture or personality that endures beyond any single leader and any single program. Organizations have enduring patterns that take on a life of their own. These patterns cause some employees to join and others to leave. These patterns become expectations of old customers and attract new customers. They give investors confidence when they support a credible business strategy.

These patterns or culture become the capabilities embedded within an organization. Most successful organizations have something they are known for that defines them; for example, Southwest Airlines is known for service and Disney theme parks for family entertainment. Firm identity should come from HR policies and practices. It needs to be developed based on a business strategy that recognizes the importance of shared culture.

A firm's identity should focus HR work on deliverables more than doables, from activity to outcome. For example, traditional measures of training are activity based (say, the percentage of managers who received forty hours of training last year) and cost based (how much was spent on training). Obviously, the more appropriate issue is what the impact was of the training received last year and its return on investment. Deliverables become the outcomes of HR activity and thus the capabilities of the organization.

In both talent-rich and talent-poor markets, HR professionals can make a major contribution by ensuring a constant flow of the right talent to the right place at the right time. HR professionals need to ensure that employees are both competent enough to do their job and committed enough to do it well. Ensuring talent requires innovative HR practices tailored to the needs of the individual employees and fair and equitable HR practices ensuring that employees who give more value get more value in return.

Organizational capabilities represent the things an organization is good at doing. With the new business realities, companies will have to identify and create new capabilities to enable them to succeed. These organization capabilities should be the deliverables of HR. They also become the intangibles that investors and customers value.

With a definition of *organization* as a set of capabilities, HR professionals can partner with line managers to assess which capabilities are critical to a firm's success. They can also help audit what the firm is and should be doing to augment these capabilities. Thus, HR professionals can play a role in deciding how the presence or absence of capabilities influences the corporation business strategy. They also can play a key role in deciding how to build new capabilities and competencies.

Performing organizational audits places new demands on HR professionals. HR professionals who established careers in a particular functional area of expertise, such as benefits or compensation, may need to learn to rethink and expand their work to focus on capabilities. As capabilities and intangibles become part of the competitive reality, HR professionals can contribute more value. They can measure their success by business success; their deliverables become the capabilities and intangibles of the firm; they can participate in key business forums where their ideas move the business forward.

Conclusion

HR is at a crossroads. There are unmistakable increased demands and opportunities for HR to add value in today's business world. HR professionals who want to add value to employees, customers, investors, and the organization must rethink their roles. The demand for HR to do more and to do different things has come about not only because HR professionals are calling for it, but also because business conditions require it. Organizations that invest in the right type of HR work will see enormous returns in terms of employee, customer, investor, and organizational results. Those that do not will have difficulty being competitive.

Because of new business realities and the need to develop a new HR value proposition, the field of HR is in flux. The rhetoric of being a business partner is being replaced by the reality that HR must add value or be eliminated. HR professionals need to focus on the ways in which this function can add value to employees, customers, investors, and the organization. This reality, which should challenge and engage HR professionals, represents a tremendous opportunity that can lead to a transformational restructuring of the HR profession and the role of HR in organizations.

Notes

1. Many have documented the transitions in HR. Some of this work includes: Effron, M., Gandossy, R., and Goldsmith, M. (eds.). (2003). *Human Resources in the Twenty-First Century.* New York: Wiley. Fitz-enz, J., and Phillips, J. (1998). *A New Vision for Human Resources: Defining the Human Resources Function by Its Results.* Fredericton, N.B., Canada: Canadian Research Institute for Social Policy Publications. Lawler, E., and Mohrman, S. (2003). *Creating a Strategic Human Resources Organization: An Assessment of Trends and New Directions.* Palo Alto, Calif.: Stanford University Press.

2. Our list of "demands" on business is not exhaustive but indicative of what business leaders are facing. We have culled this list from many sources, including our own experience with thousands of business leaders.

3. Work on the changing nature of customer-firm interactions can be found in: Rucci, A., Kirn, S., and Quinn, R. (1998). The employee-customer-profit chain at Sears. *Harvard Business Review,* Jan.-Feb., pp. 82–99. Lewis, J. (1995). *The Connected Corporation: How Leading Companies Win Through Customer-Supplier Alliances.* New York: Simon & Schuster. Whiteley, R. G. (1993). *The Customer Driven Company.* Reading, Mass.: Addison-Wesley. Zaltman, G. (2003). *How Customers Think: Essential Insights into the Mind of the Market.* Boston: Harvard Business School Press.

4. See the following: Applegate, L., Austin, R., and McFarlan, F. W. (2001). *Creating Business Advantage in the Information Age.* New York: McGraw-Hill/Irwin. Thorp, J. (2003). *The Information Paradox: Realizing the Business Benefits of Information Technology.* New York: McGraw-Hill. Luftman, J. (ed.). (2003). *Competing in the Information Age: Align in the Sand.* New York: Oxford University Press. Turban, E., McLean, E., and Wetherbe, J. (2001). *Information Technology for Management: Transforming Business in the Digital Economy.* New York: Wiley.

5. Ulrich, D., and Smallwood, N. (2003). *Why the Bottom Line Isn't.* New York: Wiley.

6. See the following: Ulrich, D. (1995). Shared services: Reengineering the HR function. *Human Resource Planning Journal,* 18(3):12–24. Schulman, D., Harmer, M., Dunleavy, J., and Lusk, J. (1999). *Shared Services: Adding Value to the Business Units.* New York: Wiley. Quinn, B., Kris, A., and Cooke, R. (2000). *Shared Services: Mining for Corporate Gold.* London: Financial Times.

7. See the following: DePamphilis, D. (2001). *Mergers, Acquisitions, and Other Restructuring Activities: An Integrated Approach to Process, Tools, Cases and Solutions.* Orlando., Fla.: Academic Press. Weston, F., and Weaver, S. (2001). *Mergers and Acquisitions.* New York: McGraw-Hill. Hitt, M., Harrison, J., and Ireland, D. (2001). *Mergers and Acquisitions: A Guide to Creating Value for Stakeholders.* New York: Oxford University Press.

8. See the following: Baruch, B., and Zarowin, P. (1999). The boundaries of financial reporting and how to extend them. *Journal of Accounting Research,* 37:353–385. Baruch, B. (2001). *Intangibles.* Washington, D.C.: Brookings Institution Press. Ernst & Young. (2000, Nov.). *Innovation Partnership Newsletter.* Eccles, R. G., Herz, R., Keegan, M., and Philips, D. (2001). *Value Reporting Revolution.* New York: Wiley.

9. See the following: Johnson, L., and Phillips, B. (2003). *Absolute Honesty: Building a Corporate Culture That Values Straight Talk and Rewards Integrity.* New York: AMACOM. Maxwell, J. (2003). *There's No Such Thing as "Business Ethics": There's Only One Rule for Making Decisions.* New York: Warner Faith.

10. Lawler, E. (2000). *Rewarding Excellence.* San Francisco: Jossey-Bass.

11. See the following: Celente, Gerald. (1998). *Trend 2000: How to Prepare for and Profit from the Changes of the Twenty-First Century.* New York: Warner Books. Judy, R., and d'Amico, C. (1997). *Workforce 2020: Work and Workers in the Twenty-First Century.* New York: Hudson Institute.

12. See the following: Bartlett, C., and Ghoshal, S. (1998). *Managing Across Borders: The Transnational Solution* (2nd ed.). Boston: Harvard Business School Press. Galbraith, J. (1995).

Designing Organizations: An Executive Briefing on Strategy, Structure, and Process. San Francisco: Jossey-Bass. Evans, P., Pucik, V., and Barsoux, J. L. (2002). *The Global Challenge: Frameworks for International Human Resource Management* New York: McGraw-Hill. Nohria, N., and Ghoshal, S. (1997). *The Differentiated Network: Organization Multinational Corporations for Value Creation.* San Francisco: Jossey-Bass.

13. The concept of capability has been discussed in: Ulrich, D., and Lake, D. (1990). *Organization Capability: Competing from the Inside/Out.* New York: Wiley. Ulrich, D. (1993). Profiling organizational competitiveness: Cultivating capabilities. *Human Resource Planning,* 16(3):1–17. Lawler, E. E. III. (1992). *The Ultimate Advantage.* San Francisco: Jossey-Bass.

14. See the following: Ashkenas, R., Ulrich, D., Jick, T., and Kerr, S. (1995). *The Boundaryless Organization.* San Francisco: Jossey-Bass. Ghoshal, S., and Bartlett, C. (1999). *The Individualized Corporation: A Fundamentally New Approach to Management.* New York: HarperBusiness. Galbraith, J. (1993). *Competing with Flexible Lateral Organization.* Reading, Mass.: Addison-Wesley.

15. The employee value proposition is laid out in Ulrich and Smallwood (2003). Lawler, E. (2003). *Treat People Right.* San Francisco: Jossey-Bass.

16. See the following: Gilmore, J., and Pine, B. J. II. (1999). *The Experience Economy.* Boston: Harvard Business School Press. Schmitt, B. (2003). *Customer Experience Management: A Revolutionary Approach to Connecting with Your Customers.* New York: Wiley. Rust, R., Zeithaml, V., and Lemon, K. (2000). *Driving Customer Equity: How Customer Lifetime Value Is Reshaping Corporate Strategy.* New York: Free Press.

17. Becker, B. E., Huselid, M. A., and Ulrich, D. *The HR Scorecard.* Boston: Howard Business School Press.

Chapter Two

New Roles for HR

There is no question that HR must change if it is to respond to the business demands identified in Chapter One. We have covered some of the opportunities that the function can capitalize on. The challenge now is to specify how HR departments—and the roles of the professionals and staff in those departments—should change. We first consider the ways in which individual HR professionals can respond to the new demands and become major contributors to the effectiveness of their organization. Then we examine how the HR function at large can be transformed. One without the other will not work: HR professionals who supply value but operate in a dysfunctional organization will not long endure. HR organizations with the right focus and agenda staffed by less-than-competent HR professionals will not endure either. Both value-adding personal roles and the right roles for HR departments are necessary if HR is to supply the value that organizations need and want.

New Roles for HR Professionals

HR professionals must be more than partners to be high-value-added professionals in organizations; they must be players. Players contribute. They are engaged. They are in the game, not observers of the game. They deliver value. They do things that make a difference. Based on our observations of HR players, we can identify six roles that HR professionals can play that contribute to their organizations' abilities to meet the demands discussed in Chapter One: strategist, coach, architect, designer and deliverer, facilitator, and leader and manager. HR players who master these six roles add value by making much-needed contributions to their organization's ability to perform effectively.[1]

HR Player as Business Strategist

An effective business strategy is the foundation on which all business activities should rest and is critical to the success of any organization. A strategy defines the organization's direction, focuses attention, sets goals, and supports the implementation of changes that ensure the goals are realized. Increasingly, the critical resources required by an organization to define and deliver its strategy are not money, materials, or even access to markets but the human capital and capabilities of the organization. The implication of this for HR professionals is clear: they must be at the table when business strategies are developed and plans for implementing those strategies are made.[2]

Participating in the formation of business strategies enables HR professionals to ensure that realistic strategies—strategies that take human capital factors into account—are developed. Sometimes aspirations exceed capacity; bold strategy statements are developed that create more cynicism than commitment because they can never be delivered. HR professionals can help shape demanding yet realistic business strategies that engender enthusiasm and confidence.

Furthermore, HR professionals as strategists may help identify business opportunities because they are aware of their organization's human capital resources and capabilities. In strategy-setting sessions, HR professionals may identify market opportunities that leverage current capabilities into new business areas. For example, Marriott has the ability to lodge and feed large numbers of people. Leveraging these core competencies has led Marriott beyond its hotel business into a vacation club business and an executive-stay business.

HR professionals should play an important role in discussions about strategy implementation because they are uniquely positioned to identify critical and sometimes intangible capabilities. They can then align HR practices to strategic goals, and mobilize resources for accomplishing the strategy. It is generally easier to declare a strategy than to accomplish one. HR professionals who bring rigor and expertise to the delivery of strategy add enormous value.

It is critical that HR players do more than just implement business strategy. They need to help formulate strategies that are based on an understanding of the human capital resources and capabilities and what the organization can do well. An observer of a business strategy session should find it difficult to identify the HR professionals in the session since they are well versed in the business and fully engaged in debating and engaging in dialogue about business issues. But over time, their questions and insights about organization and people should ensure that a better strategy is crafted and accomplished.

To be a strategist who helps both the formulation and implementation of strategy, HR professionals must learn all elements of the business. They must understand market conditions that provide opportunities, financial requirements that demand results, and core competencies and organizational capabilities that focus action. They need to be able to discuss strategy with business leaders, customers, or investors. They need to build systems that monitor results regularly.[3]

HR Player as Coach

The coach metaphor comes from music, sports, drama, and other endeavors where participants must learn, adapt, and act in an ever-improving way.[4] Coaches help participants see what does and does not work and offer counsel and advice on improving performance. Coaches focus on behaviors as well as attitudes. They have to understand individual differences and figure out how to motivate desired behavior. They know when to be critical and demanding and when to be positive and supportive. And they know how to stimulate individual behavior and encourage teamwork. Effective coaches may not be popular, but they deliver results and are accountable for the results they deliver.

HR players must be able to coach leaders about how they can build stronger organizations. They must fulfill all the duties of a good coach. As performance pressures have increased, an increasing number of CEOs have been forced out of their firm—not because they did not understand the realities of the new economy and the requirements of the organization, but because they could not build the organizational capabilities necessary to respond.[5] HR professionals can help CEOs and other leaders succeed by observing their behavior and providing feedback on how to make changes in their personal style. Too often business leaders distance themselves from both business reality and the unintended consequences of their actions. Because of their authority and position, they may not sense the impact of their decisions and actions. HR coaches are able to read their business leaders and provide them concrete feedback on their behavior. Like personal trainers, they help executives become organizationally and socially fit.

HR players are in a good position to do executive coaching because they are often outside the career politics of their organization (for example, they are not after the senior leader's job) and have training in the human side of the business. They can report on the unintended consequences of a leader's actions and offer insights not often shared with a leader. When they are not in a good position to coach a senior executive, they almost always can find someone, often an outsider, to coach the executive.

For HR professionals to coach, they must build a relationship of trust with the business leader. This relationship emerges when the HR professional expresses personal concern for the leader, empathizes with the leader's challenges, offers specific suggestions for the leader's actions, spends time with the leader both observing and sharing observations, and is willing to offer the leader feedback she or he may not receive elsewhere. In organizations, few members are willing to tell the leaders what they do not want to hear. Coaches must find ways to share good news and bad with the trust that both messages are intended to help the leader and company improve.

In order to design and deliver HR practices, HR players must be current in the theory and practice of HR. They must know what HR practices are deployed by other firms and be able to adapt those ideas to their own firm. They need to stay current through active participation in professional associations where ideas are generated and shared. They need to follow the literature and keep abreast of theory and practice. We are regularly appalled at the lack of knowledge of HR professionals in their supposed areas of expertise. For example, at a conference recently for chief learning officers, those charged with developing learning agendas for their firms, we were asked how to spell "Chris Argyris" and to recommend one of his readings; few of them could do either. We might not expect HR generalists to be cognizant of work by Argyris and other organizational learning theorists, but we would expect learning officers to be conversant with his ideas.

HR professionals need to be management scholars and researchers, constantly screening existing literature and doing research within their own firms. With good research, they can prioritize HR practices that have the greatest impact and know where to invest limited resources. They need to know how to measure the impact of the HR investments they make. They need to become experts not only at seeing what needs to be done, but at making it happen and evaluating the effectiveness of their investments.

HR Player as Facilitator

Even with good intent, most changes fall short of their promise. Personal programs for weight loss, smoking cessation, or exercise often are like New Year's resolutions that begin with enthusiasm and end with quiet fizzles. Similarly, organizational programs that begin with great fanfare all too often end up becoming fads that lack sustainability. In the new business reality, it is easy for companies to fall prey to chasing the latest fads, only to find they never improve their performance.

HR professionals as facilitators understand the process for getting things done.[8] They have the ability to make change happen and sustain that change at three levels. First, they help teams operate effectively and efficiently. Today teams and teamwork are a cornerstone in virtually all organizations, both within the boundaries of the firm and across them. HR players as facilitators ensure that all types of teams have the capacity to focus, accomplish, and function effectively. Facilitators build, coach, and sustain teamwork. Teams that work well have the capacity to leverage individual excellence and ensure collective performance. In the new business reality, teams are inevitable because no one person has access to all the knowledge and information that is needed. Teams that are managed well outperform individuals. HR facilitators ensure that teams perform well.

Second, facilitators ensure that organizational change happens. Rapid organizational responses to business needs make or break today's organizations. HR players as facilitators instill a change agenda by ensuring that organizations have the capacity and discipline to make change happen. In the new economy, being a change agent is not an option. HR facilitators have to be thought leaders and practice masters when it comes to getting organizations to change. As organizational facilitators, they bring together resources, focus attention, make sure that good decisions are made and quickly implemented.

Third, facilitators ensure that alliances operate effectively. In the new economy, knowledge does not have to be owned to be accessed. Accessing knowledge and skills through alliances such as part ownership, joint projects, partnerships, or supplier relationships is the bailiwick of the HR facilitator. Ensuring that ideas, competencies, authority, and rewards move across alliance boundaries is important for the rapid response that is required in the new economy.

In some ways facilitators are like coaches, but instead of focusing on a person, they focus on collectives of people in teams, organizations, and alliances. Like coaches, they shape points of view and offer feedback on progress. Facilitators have the more complicated task of doing so for groups of individuals, not just individuals.

To facilitate, HR professionals must learn skills in process observation. They need to be able to identify the nuances of processes, which often include issues related to influence and power. Facilitators know how to manage power and authority. In teams, organizations, and alliances, they coordinate power to ensure the authority to act. HR facilitators know how to obtain the resources needed to accomplish goals. The processes they need to master include the ability to do team building, organizational decision making, and alliance management.

HR facilitation has a legacy in organizational development (OD). In OD work, professionals help groups identify their charter and then learn how to collaborate to accomplish their charter. While some of the traditional OD work associated with personal growth has been disparaged, the need to facilitate teams, organizations, and alliances is gaining in importance.

HR Player as Leader and Manager

We have worked in companies where the senior HR leaders are strategists, coaches, architects, designers, and facilitators, but they have limited credibility because they do not effectively manage their own function. They do not practice what they preach. In these cases, business leaders often pay attention to what they see more than what they hear. Outstanding leadership of an HR function earns credibility.[9]

In a number of cases, we have seen new heads of HR appointed and immediately face the challenge of dealing with tough problems in their function. In some cases, this has meant that a disgruntled or dysfunctional employee whom the previous leader had not dealt with needed to be fired. In other cases, it has meant a need to reduce HR budget and improve the services it offers. Senior HR professionals who do not face up to and implement good business practices within their own functions lose credibility as they advocate ideas and actions to others.

In order to lead, HR players need to apply a leadership model to themselves. The definition of effective leadership that we advocate is simple and clear: getting the right results the right way. Leaders know and do things that ensure their followers do things the right way. HR leaders need to define clearly both the behaviors they should demonstrate as leaders (setting clear goals, being decisive, communicating inside and out, and managing change, for example) and the results they must deliver.

Roles for the HR Function

In order for HR professionals to play the six roles we have just discussed, the HR function itself needs to play a demanding and complex combination of roles. Table 2.1 describes three roles that HR can play.[10] The first, HR management, focuses on the administrative work inherent in HR and is where HR organizations traditionally have focused. It is essential to fulfill this role, but it is not sufficient to meet many of today's demands. The second role, business partner, is where the HR departments in large organizations are increasingly operating. It represents progress but falls short of fully addressing business strategy. The third role, strategic partner, is where HR functions need to play to fully participate in business strategy and organizational effectiveness. It does not supersede the other two but, rather, builds on them. The first two roles are necessary; thus, the third role needs to build on them and add value beyond what they allow.

Management Role

Since many recent books and articles focus a great deal on how HR can be a business or strategic partner, we worry that the administrative work will be overlooked. HR administrative work must be done, and done flawlessly at world-class cost and quality levels. In every company, employees must be hired, paid, benefits processed, roles assigned, and training offered. But administrative work cannot dominate HR and prevent it from playing a key role in business operations and business strategy. All too often in the past, it has dominated in terms of both resources and attention. The key is striking an effective balance.

Table 2.1 The Three HR Roles: Management, Business Partner, and Strategic Partner

Role	Aims	Process	Strategy
Management	Business orientation. Services provided expressed as outputs or products. Voice of the customer.	Build performance-management capabilities. Develop managers: Link competencies to job requirements and career development. Plan for succession. Enhance organizational change capabilities. Build an organization-wide HR network. Measure HR operational effectiveness.	HR (and all other functions) inspect business plans; inputs from HR may be inserted in the planning process.
Business partner	Line management owns HR as part of its role. HR is an integral member of management teams. Culture of the firm evolves to fit with strategy and vision.	Organize HR flexibly around the work to be done (programs and projects, outsourcing). Focus on the development of people and organizations (road maps, teams, organizational design). Leverage competencies, manage learning linkages; build organizational work. Redesign capabilities. Develop leadership. Measure human capital capabilities and impact of HR practices.	HR is key part of the management team.
Strategic partner	HR is a major influence on business strategy. HR systems drive business performance.	Self-service for transactional work. Transactional work outsourced. Knowledge management. Focus on organizational development. Change management. HR processes tied to business strategies. Measures of strategy implementation as well as core competencies and capabilities.	HR is key contributor to strategic planning and change management.

Table 2.2 presents data from a 2001 study of how HR functions spend their time.[11] It shows that relatively little time is spent being a business partner and HR system developer. The same study found that little has changed since 1995. It appears that HR is making slow progress at best toward meeting the needs identified in Chapter One, despite the large number of books and articles that have argued that the function needs to become a business or strategic partner. HR in large part is still behind the curve and must find ways to deliver the requisite administrative work at a world-class level while allowing for the time needed to respond to the transformational demands we identified.

Many HR organizations, in other words, have yet to undertake a serious overhaul. They have yet to find ways to deliver HR transaction work flawlessly at lower and lower costs so that they can free up time and budget dollars to contribute to organizational effectiveness by being business and strategic partners.

The cost of operating the HR department, which includes employee record keeping and salary and benefit administration—but usually not payroll processing or the cost of pay and benefits for the workforce—is typically about 1 percent of the operating expense of

Table 2.2 Percentage of Time Spent on HR Roles, 2001

Role	Time Spent
Maintaining records: Collect, track, and maintain data on employees.	14.9%
Auditing/controlling: Ensure compliance to internal operations, regulations, and legal and union requirements.	11.4
HR service provider: Assist with implementation and administration of HR practices.	31.3
Development of HR systems and practices: Develop new HR systems and practices.	19.3
Strategic business partner: Serve as member of the management team; become involved with strategic HR planning, organizational design, and strategic change.	23.2

the corporation. If we include payroll processing and assume the cost of processing paychecks is as high as ten dollars per employee per month (in the upper half of most studies), the added cost to operations is less than one-tenth of 1 percent. Viewed from another perspective, the HR administrative expense per employee typically runs from a thousand dollars to sixteen hundred dollars annually, depending on the industry.

When we consider the HR landscape, we see three approaches to accomplishing the administrative work of HR more effectively. First, we see organizations using service centers. Service centers emerged in the 1990s as a way to get administrative tasks done more efficiently in a centralized standardized way. Call centers are used to answer employee questions in a standardized way rather than by having a number of embedded HR professionals doing the same tasks in different organizational units. Service centers usually do routine, standard transactions better, faster, and cheaper.

A second approach is to do HR administrative work through self-service IT–based systems. Technology allows a great deal of administrative HR work to be done by employees themselves. Self-reliance, self-sufficiency, and employee self-service are becoming increasingly popular as HR professionals remove themselves from the operations of HR and enable employees to manage their transactions directly with the firm. Technology can streamline many of the routine transactions handled by HR, such as changing benefits and applying for jobs, and allow these transactions to be accomplished by employees and managers twenty-four hours a day, seven days a week. As employees become more technology literate and software packages become more user friendly and accessible, employees are better able to access personnel information such as policy information, retirement updates, job or career opportunities within the firm, and skill assessments.

In the third approach, HR transactional and administrative work is outsourced. Outsourcing is not new. As can be seen in Table 2.3, some HR services, such as employee assistance and benefits, are already outsourced by a significant number of firms.[12] HR outsourcing

Table 2.3 Outsourcing of HR Services

	Percentage Responding 2001			Mean		
	Not at All	Partially	Completely	1995	1998	2001
HR planning	96	4	0	1.0	1.1	1.0
Strategic planning	93	7	0	—	1.1	1.1
Organizational development	77	21	2	1.3	1.3	1.2
Organizational design	91	8	1	—	1.2	1.1
Employee training and education	26	73	2	1.6	1.9	1.8
Management development	41	59	1	1.5	1.6	1.6
HRIS	54	43	3	1.3	1.6	1.5*
Employee record keeping	73	26	1	1.2	1.4	1.3
Performance appraisal	93	6	1	1.0	1.1	1.1*
Recruitment	49	50	2	1.4	1.6	1.5*
Selection	83	17	1	1.2	1.2	1.2
Career planning	86	14	1	1.1	1.2	1.2
Benefits	19	72	9	1.7	1.9	1.9*
Compensation	55	44	1	1.2	1.5	1.5*
Legal affairs	44	51	5	1.4	1.6	1.6*
Affirmative action	68	30	2	1.1	1.2	1.3*
Employee assistance	20	26	54	—	2.2	2.3
Competency and talent assessment	68	31	1	—	—	1.3
Union relations	86	14	0	1.1	1.1	1.1

*Significant difference ($p \leq .05$) between 1995 and 2001.

has been growing on a process-by-process basis for years. Table 2.3 shows a number of significant increases from 1995 through 2001. The result is that HR executives are increasingly being put in the role of vendor manager.

Although cost is the most often talked about reason for out-sourcing, surveys tell us that other considerations are also impor-tant. Table 2.4 shows the results of a survey of why organizations outsource.[13] The most common reported reasons are employee ser-vice and accessibility to the latest technology. When the service contract is written, cost is always at the top of the list. Other com-mon themes are saving time in terms of service delivery and quality improvement as judged by errors in the process.

Overall, organizations expect that better employee service will be a natural result of outsourcing. A focus on cost and speed metrics

Table 2.4 Reasons for Outsourcing

Reason	Percentage
Most common reasons for outsourcing	
Improve HR service delivery or quality	91
Gain access to technology	74
Gain access to expertise or innovation	70
Secondary reasons for outsourcing	
Predict HR costs	36
Increase flexibility	34
Reduce administrative head count	31
Criteria least important for outsourcing	
Reduce risks	44
Redeploy and refocus HR resources	42
Reduce administrative head count	41
Top criteria incorporated in service agreement	
Predictable HR costs	76
Improved HR service delivery and quality	70
Access to technology	54

is understandable. However, this focus can suboptimize the effort if it does not look at the issue from a more strategic standpoint. The larger issue behind any significant HR improvement effort should be to accelerate the capacity of the organization to compete on the basis of human and organizational capability.

The way HR administrative work is done affects an organization's ability to use and develop its human capital. The productivity level of the workforce has much more impact on profitability than does reducing the cost of an HR administrative process. Efforts to do administrative work more efficiently should focus not just on process improvement but also on making positive changes in employee behavior, such as freeing up their time to do their jobs or making the organization a more attractive place to work.

Outsourcing profoundly affects the role and needed skill sets of the HR function. At least in the transactional areas such as employee records and benefits, outsourcing of administration changes HR's role from doers to supervisors and reduces the need for head count. Outsourcing puts HR into the role of vendor manager. In the case of small outsourcing contracts, this is not a major change, but when large multi-HR process contracts are involved, it is. These contracts involve hundreds of millions of dollars. In order to manage them effectively, HR often needs expertise in finance, contract negotiations, and HR processes.

When organizations outsource HR services, they still need to have design expertise in key HR areas. This is critical in two respects: so that HR can work with the outsourcer to be sure that the best HR processes are used; and to prevent the organization from becoming too dependent on the outsourcer. Organizations also need to evaluate vendors and, if necessary, replace them.

Any time that organizations give work over to someone else, they absorb risks. One of the greatest risks when HR is outsourced is the loss of expertise internally. As technology processes and regulations evolve, vendors build skills, but the customer, the HR department, might fall behind. The organization might also fall behind in employee relations. If the majority of contacts around transaction processes and data take place between the vendor and the employee, the organization may miss opportunities to keep its finger on the pulse of the workforce as well as demonstrating its concern for employees.

Organizational Effectiveness Expert Role

The HR function needs to be a source of expertise on key organizational effectiveness issues, such as organizational design, change management, work design, strategy development, and organizational capability development. Measurement and analytical expertise with respect to HR and organizational effectiveness are also critical; without them, HR will never be able to make the kind of data-based judgments that other parts of the organization will listen to and act on.

HR professionals with expertise in organizational development can deliver value by doing internal consulting with business units. They can provide expertise in how to develop and implement business strategies.

HR professionals can help learning and knowledge move across business units. They can create menus of knowledge resources from which business unit HR professionals select choices. They can form relationships with outside vendors that have deep knowledge and bring that knowledge into the firm. To justify their existence, HR professionals in centers of expertise often have to be even better consultants than outsiders. One way they can do this is by transferring and adopting knowledge from one business unit to another and by building relationships for sourcing knowledge from outside the company.

In some cases, specialized expertise outside an organization might help the organization gain a critical capability required for success. An internal HR professional may form an alliance with an external vendor, either an individual or team of individuals, and work with them to bring such expertise into the organization. For example, firms have used leadership development forums to help create change in their organizations. In many cases, leaders of the firm teach future leaders; in other cases, they are supplemented with external experts who provide content expertise and help bring best practices in the organization. Blurring the lines between where work is done and focusing more explicitly on the outcomes of the work can help HR professionals inside a firm collaborate with those outside to add value.

Conclusion

In order to meet the demand for HR services that comes from the new business realities facing most organizations today, HR professionals need to be attuned to business realities and deliver value beyond their traditional administrative activities. The HR function needs to find new ways to deliver basic HR services, and HR professionals need to play key roles as business and strategic partners. We have laid out some of the new roles that HR professionals might play and suggested that outsourcing HR work is a potentially effective way to get administrative work done.

Notes

1. This discussion draws heavily on the work of D. Beatty and the following articles: Ulrich, D., and Beatty, D. (2001). From partners to players: Extending the HR playing field. *Human Resource Management*, 40:293–308. Beatty, R. W., and Schneier, C. E. (1996). New HR roles to impact organizational performance: From partners to players. *Human Resource Management*, 36(1), 29–38.

2. Discussions of the HR business strategists role may be found in: Brockbank, W., and Ulrich, D. (2003). *HR Competencies for the Future*. Washington, D.C.: Society for Human Resource Management. Ulrich, D., Brockbank, W., Yeung, A., and Lake, D. (1995). Human resource competencies: An empirical assessment. *Human Resource Management Journal*, 34(4):473–496.

Ulrich, D., Brockbank, W., and Yeung, A. (1990). Beyond belief: A benchmark for human resources. *Human Resource Management*, 28:311–335.

3. Work on strategic HR competencies comes from Brockbank and Ulrich (2003).

4. Information on coaching can be found in: Hudson, F. (1999). *The Handbook of Coaching: A Comprehensive Resource Guide for Managers, Executives, Consultants, and HR.* San Francisco: Jossey-Bass. Silberman, M. (ed.). (2000). *The Consultant's Toolkit: High-Impact Questionnaires, Activities, and How to Guides for Diagnosing and Solving Client Problems.* San Francisco: Jossey-Bass/Pfeiffer. Goldsmith, M., Lyons, L., Freas, A., and Witherspoon, R (eds.). (2000). *Coaching for Leadership: How the World's Greatest Coaches Help Leaders Learn.* San Francisco: Jossey-Bass/Pfeiffer. Fitzgerald, C., and Berger, J. G. (eds.). (2002). *Executive Coaching: Practices and Perspectives.* New York: Davies-Black.

5. Dotlich, D., Charan, R., and Hogan, R. (2003). *Why CEOs Fail: The Eleven Behaviors That Can Derail Your Climb to the Top and How to Manage Them.* San Francisco: Jossey-Bass.

6. The architect metaphor has been developed by: Morabito, J., Sack, I., and Bhate, A. (1999). *Organization Modeling: Innovative Architectures for the Twenty-First Century.* Upper Saddle River, N.J.: Prentice Hall. Nadler, D., Gerstein, M., and Shaw, R. (1992). *Organizational Architecture: Designs for Changing Organizations.* San Francisco: Jossey-Bass. Nadler, D., and Tushman, M. (1997). *Competing by Design: The Power of Organizational Architecture.* New York: Oxford University Press. Nadler, D., and others. (1992). *Organizational Architecture: Designs for Changing Organizations.* San Francisco: Jossey-Bass. Lombardo, M., and Eichinger, R. (2003). *Leadership Architect Norms and Validity Report.* Minneapolis: Lominger.

7. The role of designer and deliverer of HR actions is found from many sources, including the following: Pfau, B., and Kay, I. (2001). *Human Capital Edge: Twenty-One Practices Your Company*

Must Implement (or Avoid) to Maximize Shareholder Value. New York: McGraw-Hill. Jackson, S., and Schuler, R. (2002). *Managing Human Resources Through Strategic Partnerships.* Cincinnati, Ohio: South-Western.

8. Skills in facilitation can be found in the following: Block, P. (1999). *Flawless Consulting: A Guide to Getting Your Expertise Used.* San Francisco: Jossey-Bass/Pfeiffer. Silberman. (2000). Schaffer. (1997).

9. Work on leadership as applied to HR can be found in the following: Ulrich, D., Zenger, J., and Smallwood, N. (2001). *Results Based Leadership.* Boston: Harvard Business School Press. Lombardo, M., and Eichinger, R. (2002). *The Leadership Machine.* Minneapolis: Lominger. Zenger, J., and Folkman, J. (2002). *The Extraordinary Leader.* New York: McGraw-Hill. Goldsmith, M., Bennis, W., and O'Neil, J. (2003). *Global Leadership: The Next Generation.* London: Financial Times/Prentice Hall.

10. Based on Lawler, E., and Mohrman, S. A. (2003). *Creating a Strategic Human Resources Organization.* Palo Alto, Calif.: Stanford University Press.

11. Based on Lawler and Mohrman (2003).

12. Based on Lawler and Mohrman (2003).

13. Based on Yeh, V. (1999). *Outsourcing Survey.* Saratoga, Calif.: Saratoga Institute and Andersen Consulting.

Chapter Three

Evaluating the Effectiveness of HR

The use of quantitative measures and metrics in human capital management is a recent, but long-overdue, development. Without measurement, it is impossible to determine how effective most programs, practices, and strategies are. Measures of HR are fundamental to the successful movement of HR into the roles we discussed in Chapter Two. Without accurate measurement, it is impossible to determine how successful HR is in its administrative role, and without measurement, the case for HR's becoming a strategic player is particularly difficult, if not impossible, to make.

Reduced to their essentials, measures are simply numbers that describe an amount of something, such as cost or time. A metric is a definition of a specific process or outcome such as the cost per hire. HR professionals may say they add value, but because of the lack of metrics, they are often unable to support this argument. Furthermore, they are unable to make data-based decisions about which of their programs work and how well they work. Perhaps most important, they are unable to contribute analyses based on HR data when business decisions are made. Metrics are also important to decisions concerning the structure of the HR function. It is impossible to make high-quality decisions about such issues as what to outsource, how effective outsourcing is, and how to allocate an HR budget without good measures of the cost and effectiveness of HR programs and activities.

Measurement Areas

Despite the potential value of measurement and metrics, we estimate that as many as 75 percent of HR departments do not have a comprehensive, effective measurement system. In short, HR tracking and measuring is important but not practiced. As HR moves into new professional and managerial roles, metrics must move at the same time. For example, as HR moves into the role of managing vendors, metrics that assess service delivery and cost are vital; otherwise, it is impossible to write performance-based vendor contracts and assess vendor performance.

The good news is that more executives and HR directors are coming to accept that meaningful human capital management metrics can be designed and reported. There also is a growing recognition of the importance of using analytic models to determine just how effective HR practices and programs are and how much of an impact they have on organizational performance.

The Foundation

Quantification of any business activity, including HR management, can, and in most cases should, include five types of measures:

- Cost of the unit of product or service delivered
- Cycle time of the process from inception to completion
- Volume or quantity produced
- Quality or error rate
- Human reaction to the process or result

The first three are objective. There is no judgment involved in measuring them. The last two are subjective in that the stakeholders, employees and customers, determine how well the process or result suits their needs. Measurements can be taken at any point in a process or at the end of a process.

To obtain the greatest utility, agreement is needed on what to include in each of the measures. For example, an organization that wants to determine the cost of a process such as hiring or training has to decide which activities and resources are to be included or excluded from the definition of that process. Direct out-of-pocket costs such as fees paid to vendors should be included, but what about the cost of staff time in carrying out the process? There is no accounting rule that determines what to include. However, when the users of the process agree on the elements to include, a common language can be formed, around which later evaluations can be made.

There are abundant opportunities to apply cost, quantity, timeliness, quality, and employee reaction metrics to determine the quality of HR administrative services. Measuring their effectiveness is required for HR. Without measurement, it is impossible for HR to operate like a business and decide how to deliver its services. However, quantitative and qualitative measurement can be more than just a tool to assess administrative services. Measurement is an enabler that can help position the HR department as a strategic contributor to organizational effectiveness. As we pointed out in Chapter Two, HR has more than one role to fill. From administrator to strategic business partner, HR has many opportunities to contribute positively to the effectiveness of the organization as well as the satisfaction and growth of employees.

Quantitative methods can be applied to all roles, from transactional to strategic. However, there is a difference in the application among the roles. In transactional activities, mostly direct, internal measures of HR efficiency should be used. In strategic activities, the effects of HR programs on operational and enterprise-level goals must be considered.

Transaction Management

Typically, the application of metrics to HR starts at the transactional level. Every HR practice begins with some exchange or transaction. All processes within a function can be programmed to yield data on cost, time, and quantity. The elements of a transaction include one or more persons plus resources, such as material, equipment, and energy.

Once the elements to be tracked are determined, the number of transactions and the unit cost of each can be easily programmed into the process. In many cases, a standard cost is associated with repetitive tasks to obviate the need to track the cost of each instance. Date and time inputs will eventually yield cycle time data. Given the arrival of extraction tools, the totals and averages at the end of a period are as close as a click on a mouse. The traditional administrative activities of the HR function lend themselves to the use of transaction and cost measures. HR administrative outsourcing contracts, in fact, often specify an expected level of transaction costs, time cycles, and volumes.

In HR services, the average cost per employee hired, salary action, benefit claim, counseling session, training class, or relocation can be monitored over time against predetermined standards of performance. The same method applies to process time cycles for hiring, payroll and benefit claims processing, counseling sessions, and training design and delivery. Some software programs, such as applicant tracking systems, offer automated methods for collecting volume, time, and cost data. This method can be applied to any HR transaction. Even employee relations activities such as number and type of counseling sessions can be monitored. The key question is, What is worth measuring? Over time, data on administrative efficiency can help pinpoint problem areas as well as achievements that are ordinarily lost in the daily activity. They also can help determine the best approach to performing most administrative functions.

Organizational Effectiveness

While at one level we need to know how efficiently HR processes are being managed, the more important issue is what difference they make in organizational performance. The reason for any function is found in its effect on the organization. Organizations establish HR departments not only to process newly hired employees, pay, benefits, and training, but to add value to the enterprise directly or indirectly. This has been a stumbling block for countless HR practitioners. Although they can generate improvements in costs, response times, and outputs per person, as well as quality levels and employee reactions, they have difficulty proving they translate into economic value for the organization.

Key Metrics

Standard definitions of the many HR metrics were developed in the 1980s by the Saratoga Institute in concert with the Society for Human Resources Management.[1] From this long list, a shorter, more manageable cluster of key metrics has been extracted. These key metrics are often reported in groups that focus on certain HR department activities and in macro measures of organizational factors. Some of the most common metrics in these two areas are presented in Table 3.1.

Each organization needs to develop a slate of metrics to meet its unique needs. The major value of working from a standard set is the ability to benchmark against others. Learning how internal performance compares with others in the same industry or locale is an important basis for deciding what to outsource and whether to change certain processes.

Table 3.1 Commonly Used HR and Organizational Metrics

Metrics for HR Departments	Metrics for Organizational Factors
Accession rate	Revenue per employee
Cost per each employee hired	Human capital value added
Time to fill jobs	Human capital return on investment
Benefit claims response time	Compensation versus operating expense
Training hours produced	Health care costs
Number trained	Training cost as percentage of payroll
HR expense per employee	Voluntary separation rate
HR full-time-equivalent ratio	Contingent versus regular employees

Normative Values

The interpretation of metrics needs to vary by industry, region, company size, and sometimes growth rate. Some metrics such as hiring are heavily influenced more by the local labor market and economic conditions than by other factors. Overall, the cost of hiring exempt personnel has grown very gradually but steadily for the past fifteen years. Pay and benefits tend to follow industry standards as well as company size. Pay rates change very slowly, while benefits, especially health care costs, are more volatile.

Young, aggressive, fast-growing companies typically spend little on training and more on total compensation than do large, established organizations. People-intensive industries spend more on management development, and capital-intensive companies spend more on operator and technical training. Separation rates mirror economic factors but tend to follow industry rates. The one statement regarding normative values that can be made with confidence is that trends are generally slow moving. Except when violent economic swings occur, values typically do not change more than 5 percent from year to year.

There are no normative metric values that transcend industry or regional differences. Service businesses are quite different from petrochemical and heavy manufacturing. In the U.S., western, especially Pacific Coast, normative values are dissimilar to those from the plains states and South.

Purpose of Measurement

Measurement can be performed for a variety of purposes and audiences. It can be used to determine the effectiveness of different approaches to structuring the HR function. In the case of outsourcing, a legitimate and common question that business and HR leaders ask is: "Is outsourcing the right thing to do?" With a set of standard metrics in place, we can begin to answer this question. By examining both the HR and organizational factors, we can determine if an improvement opportunity exists, and later we can monitor to determine if outsourcing has the desired affect.

Measurement also offers an opportunity for improvements in HR contribution to business performance by focusing HR managers on strategic issues, core competencies, organizational capabilities, and business transformation. Finally, it can have a major effect on employee perceptions of management's concern for them, which means that it can affect retention and organizational culture.

Measurement of the effectiveness of administrative services can be simple. We can count the volume of activity and cycle times of key processes and various costs. We can compare internal results with the performance levels in other companies. We can assess improvement by looking at historical levels of performance.

Evaluating alternative approaches to delivering administrative services becomes quite complex if the focus is on their effects on the strategic issues of employee performance and competitive advantage in the marketplace. At this point, measurement becomes multifaceted and interdependent, and the goals transcend operational objectives. We are looking for effects on strategic business issues: improving organizational capabilities and core competencies, employee retention, strategy development and implementation, market share, and return on capital. In short, we are after competitive advantages that go beyond the cost of HR administration.

Measurement Principles

Some executives and, yes, some HR professionals find the measurement of human capital a great mystery, even an unnecessary nuisance. For them, the veil that shrouds the value and ease of measurement can be lifted by the application of two fundamental principles: make it visible, and give it context.

Make It Visible

Anything can be measured if there is an operational definition. When we describe a phenomenon through visible examples, we can find measurable points. Concepts such as effectiveness, leadership, or morale can be quantitatively measured when there are operational definitions that include visible activities, behaviors, or results.

Give It Context

Measures must have a context in order to be useful. They must have a focal point, that is, corporate goals or business unit objectives, to give them relevance. Measurement alone is extra work with no value unless it is connected to a meaningful end point. Data have little utility until they are tied to an objective. This is why volume counts usually have little value by themselves. A particular number of something means nothing unless it can be viewed over time and related to a value-adding objective.

An effective measurement system tracks activity across the five types of measures: cost, time, volume, quality, and reaction. It contains the data necessary to answer any question, but it does not mean that all five types of measures are used in every situation. The relevance of any metric is its connection to the objective of the activity measured. As an example, if the corporate goal is to speed product to market, then measures of timeliness in human capital management, such as time to fill jobs or time to deliver needed training, are important. If a strategic business unit's objective is to reduce operating expense, then measures of human capital costs, such as salary budgets and cost of hiring, are appropriate.

The fifth measure, reaction, refers to the human component. It measures how someone feels about something. Examples are line manager attitudes toward HR services, employee job satisfaction or morale, and customer satisfaction. Quite often a change in one metric is the result of or correlates with a change in another metric. This is where analytics and causal models come into play. They can help HR professionals use measures to improve organizational effectiveness because they provide "what to do" results. When the number of errors in processing increases, the cost of producing that product or service increases. When the time to fill jobs moves up or down, turnover costs and employee productivity are affected. In the end, changes in any of the five measures can affect the three fundamentals of business: productivity, quality, and service.

Cost Drivers: Inside and Outside

Typically, administrative services improvement efforts focus on measures of the reduction of the unit cost of processing, producing, or delivering a product or service. It is referred to as a transaction cost. We can measure the cost of a salary action, a benefit claim, or a change to an employee record or any item that is passing through a given process.

Cost accounting has been doing transaction cost calculations for decades. Of late, activity-based costing (ABC) has become popular. The unit cost of a product or service can be determined using a recognized methodology. ABC is particularly effective at finding the hidden costs of each step in a process. This method looks at the process rather than just the individual cost items. A process change will affect the cost of individual items.

An examination of the total process of switching from one method of delivering administrative service to another usually uncovers a large number of costs. These costs are usually lumped, and often lost, under the cost of implementation and integration (I&I). In cases of sophisticated software programs, I&I costs often exceed the cost of the software by a large margin. The full costs mirror the system budget plus. They include labor, material, facilities and equipment, and energy. Total cost depends on the size and scope of the functions to be outsourced.

One way to run a cost-benefit analysis of the outsourcing of administrative services is to start by uncovering and listing the cost of the current system on an annual basis. Assume, for example, that the projected budget shows $90 million for labor, material, facilities, equipment, and energy for the functions that will be outsourced. A skeptic might ask if we always come in on budget or if overruns are more the case. In either case, in addition to the annual budget for the to-be-outsourced HRIS processes, we should add any unaccounted-for IT support such as liaison staff and corporate mainframe expense. We also may need to add in the use of real estate to house the HR employees. Taken together, these constitute the true annual cost. This is the number that should be compared to the cost of outsourcing.

To find the total transformation costs, we start with the vendor's proposed cost and then ask if any hidden costs will occur. Will personnel from other departments have to commit resources or make adjustments to their systems to accommodate the change? This can include changes in forms and the training necessary to execute them. Will rank-and-file employees have to be briefed or trained and supported through the implementation? One might even add in an error factor to acknowledge that learning curve costs will occur. These hidden costs are often missed. One caution, however, is not to nitpick ad nauseam. This can be avoided by grouping a number of minute costs into a single cost factor (for example, miscellaneous) that represents a very small percentage of the total.

During implementation and integration, costs accrue on both sides. That is, the customer must dedicate people and their related costs to the conversion at the same time as the vendor does. Vendor costs will be visible through periodic billing. Customer costs are less obvious. During implementation and integration, additional temporary staff might be required to assist with record transfers or other tasks. Finally, an oversight cost factor for management to supervise implementation can be added. As the implementation progresses, the customer should be able to withdraw resources gradually, to the point of simply managing the vendor's contract. In the end, the objective is to have an outsourced system that provides a more effective service for employees at a lower unit cost.

Time Factors: Cycle Time

One of the things the customer wants to know about any new process or product is how long it will take to convert to the new system. This is the grossest measure of time: process conversion or implementation time. This is a very important metric for the customer because conversions inevitably affect employee service and are costly. New routines don't always work right the first time, and people who are not yet accustomed to the routine can fail to respond efficiently or effectively.

At the microlevel, results that are visible shortly after an activity occurs are the easiest to measure. This is most often the case in daily process management. The number of items processed in a given time frame can be monitored before, during, and after the implementation and reported throughout the conversion period. The items can be physical such as benefit claims or interactions such as employee calls. Administrative managers live with these metrics because their performance is often judged by such numbers. It is not unusual to see cycle times increase during a conversion process. As people on both sides learn the best way to run the process, throughput times often expand until the implementation takes root.

At the process level are several possible metrics to track:

- Time to respond to requests for service
- Time to fulfill the request
- System-up time average
- Time to repair breakdowns in the system

The strategic issues in time measurement deal principally with the utilization of executive and upper-level management time. As senior people trade their daily involvement with process supervision for an oversight role, they can turn that extra time into more-value-adding work. The value of having additional time to spend on issues of employee morale, market analysis, customer service, product innovation, quality improvement, business strategy, and change management is difficult to track. But it offers potentially greater returns than improving the costs of administrative processes.

How much time managers need to spend dealing with outsourcers is likely to vary depending on the newness of the contracts, the scope of the outsourcing relationship, and the number of outsource contracts. As a general rule, the more contracts there are and the newer they are, the more time managers will need to spend managing vendors.

Volume: Amount of Output

Quantity or volume is the simplest of measures: it is just counting. What makes it a useful measure is the relationship of the amount of output to the amount of input and the relevance of the output to a goal or objective. Of course, time and quality matter, and cost is a direct function of the input-output ratio. But the only way to talk about measurement is one factor at a time. After each item is clear, then it is possible to discuss interaction effects.

Employee productivity is a function of the ratio of resource inputs to the timeliness of quality outputs. Management allocates funds for material, facilities, equipment, and employee training and supervision in the hope of obtaining more product or service and higher quality at a lower cost in a given time period. Whether one is pushing pieces of steel, paper, or people through a process, all are truly transforming something. Information is material in the form of electronic pulses rather than carbon atoms. Instead of measuring the number of I-beams or tons of newsprint produced, we can talk about the number of claims processed, the number of customer calls handled, or the number of jobs filled. In all cases, we are assuming acceptable quality. If there are defects in the steel or paper or errors in the claims or number of employees hired, the process recycles, and the volume handled goes up.

In HR outsourcing, the vendor contracts to process a certain quantity during a given time period, such as a day, week, month, quarter, or year. This is the easiest metric to monitor since it is a simple volume count. The key is to look at it along with measures of quality and employee satisfaction.

Errors: The Quality Issue

No one expects or will promise perfect quality. Hardware and software malfunctions and human errors or misunderstandings all contribute to the defect rate. Errors or defects in the deliverables are always annoying and sometimes critical. This is what spawned the Total Quality Management movement in the 1980s.

If the HR data being processed are sensitive for any reason, an error can cause significant problems. The best example of this is medical information regarding an employee. If a record is omitted or contains errors, it could be life threatening, so quality is paramount. In matters such as a botched address, miscalculated paychecks, or benefit claim checks, errors can affect an employee's cash balance. Since many people live from paycheck to paycheck, a lost or erroneous automatic payroll deposit can cause employees to overdraw their checking account. In this case, no one dies; nevertheless, the error can be significant if, for example, it angers employees and disrupts their work as they spend time trying to correct the problem.

Process error rates can be tracked in various ways. They can be counted, put into a ratio of errors per 1,000 times processed, or treated as a percentage. There is no prescribed standard. Whatever suits the customer is what should be used.

The question around any type of measure is, "So, what difference does it make?" Is it a matter of inconvenience or something more serious? In the case of HR administration, errors can be very important. They can lead to legal problems as well as the loss of human capital. Thus, measuring them is essential, in particular when HR administrative services are being evaluated.

Reactions: The Human Element

Reaction is a measurement of how someone feels about either the process or the result. Employees react to how something is handled, as well as to the result. In some cases, the how is more important than the what. A person might obtain the information he or she needs yet be very unhappy with the manner in which it was obtained. Both process and result are employee satisfaction issues. Satisfaction is a function of expectation versus realization.

All of us have experienced problems with service. We want both the process of obtaining the service and the deliverable to be acceptable. Customers are much more demanding today than they were in decades past when the pace of life was slower and technology was not so advanced. Whereas we once were satisfied to receive something in a week, today we often expect to receive it almost instantaneously. Electronic wizardry in the form of computers and the Internet has raised expectation levels to almost unattainable levels. Vendors are under pressure to respond not only quickly and accurately but also in a pleasant and helpful manner.

Reactions can be measured using surveys.[2] They can also be obtained through focus group meetings or on an ad hoc basis whereby employees send messages directly to the vendor or the HR department. In the case of administrative services, a performance metric can be established with respect to a specified annual employee satisfaction level. This might be expressed as, for instance, 98 percent. The metric can be obtained as part of a standard employee attitude survey.

The most important issue concerning employee satisfaction is the "So what?" question. What difference does it make if there is a high level of dissatisfaction? Employee unhappiness often is associated with turnover, low quality, and poor customer service. Disgruntled employees spend time complaining to each other, slowing down work processes, and taking unnecessary "sick" days. In the long run, employee commitment can erode if management does not deal with dissatisfaction. It is often important to analyze what the actual impact of satisfaction is on behavior and determine the cost of that to the organization. Although satisfaction with administrative services may not have a large impact on overall employee satisfaction, it can have an effect.

Measurement of Intangibles

The measurement of intangibles first attracted attention in the IT arena. As automated data processing became more prevalent in the 1960s and 1970s, managers looked for ways to measure the productivity of their professional and technical staffs. Initially, they applied production metrics, such as number of lines of code. It quickly became clear that more code does not equate with higher productivity. The principle is that merely counting something does not make it relevant and that more is not always good.

The counting error persists today in many HR departments, where they count the number of interviews, employees hired, salary actions, benefit claims processed, and people trained or counseled as indexes of effective human capital management. Actually they are implied measures of process costs, not value added. As with the number of people with M.B.A.s or the number of minorities in management, the mere number of anything does not necessarily indicate value. Numbers such as these may be indexes of the condition of an organization, but they are not necessarily signs of economic value added.

A number of important intangibles are susceptible to quantitative measurement and analysis. These include culture, knowledge management and organizational learning, leadership, and employer brand. Many organizational capabilities such as speed to market and product quality can be measured.

The decision to service employees from inside versus outside sources is as much a cultural as an operational or financial decision. In one instance we are aware of, an executive decided not to outsource payroll because he believed that accurate pay processing was an obligation of the corporation. Outsourcing can touch knowledge management since it is dependent on easy access to accurate data about employee skills, and it can be aided when HR executives have time to focus on it.

Since the decision to use outsourcing involves trade-offs among costs, employee service, and data control, the values of top executives come into play. Being or becoming an employer of choice can be affected by the decision to outsource. Recurring problems with the outsource provider's service can taint an organization's reputation as a good place to work. Although each of the intangibles is complex, it is not impossible or even impractical to measure their degree of value.

It is not easy to bridge the gap between the transaction processing of employee data and an intangible enterprise variable. There is no way to prove a causal connection because we cannot do experiments with control groups. Nonetheless, good answers often can be found through tracing the chain of events from changes in HR service levels to changes in employee dissatisfaction and job behavior.

It is important to consider all of the major events in the corporate mix, isolate their effect on the variable in question, and then trace changes in transaction processing to see if there are concomitant changes in the dependent variable. This exercise might show changes that parallel each other but do not cause each other; they are simply coincidental. On the other hand, we might be able to infer from the data that there probably was some causation. Our experience with senior management is that they are more susceptible to a logical argument than to the statistical analysis of causation. Every day they make huge investments based on data that are incomplete or questionable as far as causation is concerned.

Lag and Lead Indicators

The vast majority of business measures are derived from the accounting system and operational phenomena. In its most basic sense, accounting tells what was spent, what is left in the treasury, and what is owed. Operational reports provide information on how much of something passed through the organization. It traces the inputs, processes, and outputs. Marketing, sales, and service data deal with the reactions of people outside the organization: the marketplace of customers, competitors, and suppliers. As such, they all describe the past. Only in marketing is much attention paid to the future.

HR reports focus primarily on past expenses. How many transactions took place? How many people were interviewed, hired, trained, paid, provided with benefits, and given various forms of personal assistance? Every one of these metrics is about what happened rather than what is most likely to happen in the future. These data, called lag indicators, are useful as a management report card but don't point to what might be coming.

Lead indicators are generated when there is a recognition and understanding of how certain internal and external data can influence or predict future events. For the wise person, they point out how human capital should be managed in order to ensure positive results in the future.[3] Examples of lead indicators are:

- Turnover of employees in key positions
- Bench strength in key positions
- Competency levels in emerging technologies
- Ability to respond quickly to change
- Employee commitment to corporate vision and mission
- Participation in training and education opportunities
- Availability of qualified labor
- Consumer sentiment surveys
- Governmental legislation trends
- Capability of top leadership

The issue is how the HR function measures, analyzes, affects, and reacts to such indicators. Potentially, it can have an impact on lead indicators in a positive or negative way. In the best cases, it can improve them and, as a result, prevent problems and produce better organizational performance.

Conclusion

Competitive advantage comes from the leverage that results when something works well. Sometimes it is difficult to see the source of advantage when dealing with HR transactions. In manufacturing when an error is made, there are very visible consequences. Useful material turns to scrap. Since piles of defective hard goods such as steel, wood, rubber, or plastic are more visible than pieces of paper in a wastebasket or data errors on a computer screen, the error or defect is more obvious.

In addition, since cost accounting has figured material costs into the unit cost of a finished piece and because material costs are higher in manufacturing than in administrative transactions, the problem is greater. Nevertheless, because a flawed administrative function often affects employee behaviors, the loss of employee commitment, although somewhat invisible, can have a greater negative effect than a short-term increase in the unit cost of a finished piece. Material goods have no memories, but employees and customers do.

The potential value added by changes in how the HR function operates is measurable at both the tactical and strategic levels. The five measures of business activity—cost, time, volume, quality, and reaction—are applicable at both levels. The difference is that as in moving from immediate process changes to longer-term enterprise or market effects, the link is not as immediate or obvious.

Value takes many forms, from purely financial to primarily humanitarian. Each has its place, and each provides a different point of view. A composite set of metrics helps to more truly understand what is happening to an organization today, as well as how prepared it is for tomorrow.

Without metrics, it is difficult to understand when change is needed and what the effects are when major organizational changes are made. With metrics, it is not only possible to understand change, but it may be possible to influence and perhaps even control the future. Thus, in analyzing how to organize the HR function, we need to focus on the metrics that indicate how its performance and the organization's performance are affected by its structure and practices.

Notes

1. Saratoga Institute. (1985–2001). *Human Resource Benchmark Reports*. Saratoga, Calif.: Saratoga Institute.
2. Fitz-enz, J., and Davison, B. (2002). *How to Measure Human Resources Management*. (3rd ed.) New York: McGraw-Hill.
3. Fitz-enz, J. (2000). *The ROI of Human Capital*. New York: AMACOM.

Chapter Four

Design of the HR Function

The ability of an organization to deliver products and services depends heavily on its structure. In order to deliver new products and services, most organizations need to be redesigned in ways that significantly change key features of their structure. The same goes for parts of organizations. The structure of departments, functions, and operating groups within corporations determines how effective they are at meeting the demands of their internal customers and producing the kinds of products and services that the organization needs in order to be effective. The implication for HR is obvious: the function needs to be restructured because the demands on it are changing.

The restructuring of HR should begin with the way in which the traditional transactional work of HR is performed. We have already identified the new roles that HR professionals can take in organizations. We have also identified some of the ways in which the function can become a strategic partner to the organization at large. The first step toward achieving all of those goals is to excel at the administrative work.

That may seem like a letdown given the potential transformation we have been describing in the previous chapters. But there are two important reasons to start with a focus on transactional work. First, doing a good job of HR administration is a powerful way to demonstrate that the HR function is itself an effective business that knows how to meet customer demands, understands how to manage costs, and is capable of operating as an effective customer-focused organization. Chapter Three focuses on HR measures and metrics for an important reason: proof of effective delivery of traditional services provides the function with the kind of credibility that can enable HR to gain a seat at the table when key business strategy issues are being decided.

Second, good HR administration involves gathering data and analyzing human capital. These data can be of enormous help in guiding an organization's business decisions. Knowing turnover rates among key contributors and being able to identify where key skills are in an organization, for example, can be a big aid to organizations in their business activities. These and a host of other valuable insights into an organization's human capital can be developed by mining HR data.

Just as the finance function can have a large influence on corporate decisions because it is able to mine data, HR can have an influence on business when it has the kinds of data that are helpful from a business, operations, and strategy perspective. Without data, HR is forced to argue for its position from a point of view, not fact, and as a result it is unlikely to be heard. With valid, relevant data, it can much more effectively address key business issues. HR needs data that assess its own practices as well as other organizational practices to be sure that they are producing a reasonable return on investment. In order to be a player when it comes to business strategy, it needs data on human capital capabilities and on how effectively human capital is managed, allocated, and organized.

Structure of the HR Function

Traditionally, HR has been organized by function (staffing, training, payroll, pension, and so forth). Data are collected and decisions made in each of these separate functions rather than in an integrated manner. Doing more efficient administrative HR work requires integrated, not piecemeal, administrative processes. Thus, efficient HR administration is an activity that does not fit well into the traditional structure of the HR department. Too often in the traditional structure, data gathered with respect to different HR activities are not aggregated in order to provide an accurate and comprehensive view of individuals or of the organizational situation with respect to human capital.

Since HR data typically rest in separate data sets and in separate programs that do not communicate with each other, integration is difficult. For example, a staffing operation might build a competency model and collect data suggesting that employees need to be hired who have skills A, B, and C. Then the training function does an assessment and decides that employees need to develop skills C, D, and E. And the compensation function builds an appraisal and reward system encouraging employees to develop skills C, F, and G. In this case, there is some overlap on what is required (skill set C) but great diversity in required skills. In addition, there is no economy of scale in doing the assessments and making investments to improve the organization.

Departments in the traditional HR function have responsibility for both transactions and the design and management of particular HR programs. Program design and program administration require different skills and often do not fit together well in the same group. What does fit together well are the kinds of transactions that occur in hiring, benefits administration, compensation, training enrollment, and other HR administration areas. These are all high-volume transactions where economies of scale can be achieved, and well-developed, rigorous processes are needed. The obvious recommendation is that these activities be grouped together in an HR administrative function that handles high-volume transactions. It also should develop an integrated library or warehouse of HR data that can be analyzed in order to answer key strategic questions.

Over the past decade, a number of organizations have changed the internal structure of their HR organization to what might be called a front-back organization. Reporting to the HR vice president are a number of HR generalists who are assigned to the various business units or departments of the organization. In each of these business or organizational units, HR professionals work directly with line managers to monitor HR service delivery, clarify HR strategy, perform organizational audits, and make HR decisions that support the business.

Business unit HR professionals are often called relationship managers, HR partners, engagement managers, HR generalists, or just HR vice presidents. In addition to reporting to the corporate vice president of HR, they also report to the general manager or vice president of the unit for which they are responsible. They play the business partner role described in Chapter Two: coach for the business leaders, architect of a social organization, facilitator of change, and designer of the HR practices and policies.

HR generalists manage the vendors who deliver HR services to their unit. They tailor HR services and work with business leaders to create an effective organization. They coach business leaders, act as architects for specific organizational strategies, and help managers make informed HR choices. When they operate as business partners, they draw on corporate staff HR groups for in-depth expertise in HR systems and organizational effectiveness.

Whereas HR generalists work in business units, HR specialists are organized into corporate centers of expertise. The corporate center typically has a center of expertise for the key areas in the HR function, for example, compensation, organizational development, and training. These centers of expertise report to the corpo-rate HR vice president. In some cases, they must be self-supporting in the sense that they must be able to bill for the project work they do with business units.

In addition to the centers of expertise, organizations often have one or more service centers that do most of the administrative work for the HR function. A few outsource the administrative work to an HR BPO. They report to the HR vice president and in some cases have a reporting relationship to the HR generalists in the business units. Both the outsourcers and the service center population have as their major roles serving the employees in the business units.

Historically, much of the work done in service centers involved call centers, as well as the processing of forms and handling various kinds of paperwork and data entry. But as we mentioned in Chapter Two, things do not have to be done this way. An increasing number of transactions can be and are done in a self-service mode using Web-based software systems.[1] There are a number of compelling arguments for adopting an e-enabled self-service approach to HR administration. These include freeing up the internal staff to be business partners, cost reductions because of substituting technology for labor, and improvements in quality and speed. There are also some ways in which a self-service approach can help HR with its business and strategic partner roles.

Role of Information Technology

Exhibit 4.1 illustrates the relationship between information technology and the three major roles that HR can play in contributing to the management of human capital in the modern corporation.[2] These three roles range along a continuum from contributing to the company's strategy—highly uncertain, experience-based knowledge work requiring expert judgment—to transactional service work emphasizing production efficiency and service standards reflecting ease of use, responsiveness, and accuracy. The three HR roles entail different expertise, different mixes of routine or nonroutine knowledge work, and different IT tools. This is particularly true of transactions in comparison to the other two.

Routine Personnel Services

As shown in Exhibit 4.1, the greatest overlap between IT and HR occurs in the personnel services role, which involves the transactional parts of HR, such as benefits enrollment, claims, payroll, and address changes. By using IT for these transactional processes and by fostering employee self-service, HR can eliminate the multiple-step paperwork that consumes employee time as well as service center time. Much of this activity can be done by employees on a Web-based system. They can do it whenever they have free time, and no one in the service center needs to handle their paperwork.

Even with the most advanced IT systems, there is a need for some personally delivered knowledge-based services. Often this work can

Exhibit 4.1   Information Technology and HR Management

Strategic Partner	Business Support	Personnel Services
Data analysis modeling, and simulation capabilities	HR system administration employee and manager, tools, information, and advice Data and analysis tools	Transactional self-service processes
Business strategy input HR strategy formulation Strategy implementation Change management Organizational design Upgrading analytic capabilities	HR system development, learning, and improvement Consultation Talent strategy and processes Program and system upgrades	Help-line services Program and system upgrades

Note: The shaded portions show IT HR-enabled areas.

be done by call centers or help lines that deal with complex cases, answer questions, and teach employees how to use the IT systems. Over time the expectation is that there will be less and less need for personally delivered services. Better software, as well as more knowledgeable users, eventually should lead to the virtual elimination of personally delivered services.

Developing and operating electronic HR (e-HR) systems involves a high level of skill and knowledge. Developing systems that are user friendly and accurate and yield the right data requires HR system knowledge and software system design knowledge. Once a system is designed, operating it requires expertise in managing IT and the ability to change the system as the business changes.

Overall, e-HR systems are expensive to develop and maintain, but they can produce significant savings. Transaction processing is a volume business; significant savings in unit costs are greatest when the cost of product development, operations, and maintenance can be spread over a large number of users.

Business Support

Listed in the middle column of Exhibit 4.1 is the HR work involved in developing and administering HR systems and services that support the execution of the company's business strategy and, more generally, its daily business operations. These activities include the design and management of systems to secure needed talent, compensate and motivate people, train and develop them, and place people in the right jobs. They also include internal consultation to line managers about their HR needs, questions, and issues. These knowledge areas are the ones where HR departments feel most comfortable about their own capabilities and performance.

Many aspects of HR systems concerned with compensation, talent management, and training can be codified and automated. Once defined, they are amenable to self-service. For example, computer modeling tools that embed the parameters of the compensation system can be provided to managers so they can do their own compensation planning, often without the involvement of HR professionals.

Much of the role that HR has traditionally played in consulting to managers about HR issues can also be handled by putting information and tools on the Web. For example, a manager dealing with the potential transfer of an employee might find procedures, criteria, and a diagnostic set of questions on the Web to help in determining whether a transfer is desirable and exactly what needs to be done to carry out the transfer.

The development and improvement of HR systems, whether they are automated or not, entails the application of a deep understanding of the principles, regulatory issues, and dynamics of HR systems, especially if systems are to be crafted to support the strategy and the work of the organization. There needs to be a close relationship between the way the work of employees is designed and the nature of supportive HR systems such as job grades, career tracks, and incentive methods. Therefore, the crafting of effective HR systems cannot be accomplished without deep expert knowledge, and thus it frequently involves consultants.

Although much of the work involved in crafting HR systems is knowledge based and judgmental, IT tools remain relevant even in this area. Automation of HR systems and transactions makes possible the systematic tracking and evaluation of various systems, such as in determining the relationship between compensation awards and performance evaluation results. Data-based analyses, tracking, and modeling capabilities can provide a future basis for improving HR systems. These capabilities involve knowledge-oriented tools that are critical to HR's role and effectiveness in the future.

Shown at the bottom of the middle column of Exhibit 4-1 is the need for a new kind of expertise: programming and upgrading the automated systems that are required to operate effectively in a business support and execution role. This is an area where considerable IT knowledge is required, particularly when it comes to developing new systems that fit changing business strategies, new organizational designs such as virtual and network organizations, and the redesign of work systems for greater employee involvement.

Strategic Partner

The left column of Exhibit 4.1 shows the strategic partner role, which entails providing strategic advice and expertise. This includes contributing to the organization's business strategy consideration of human capital issues and playing a key leadership role in developing organizational capabilities so that the strategy can be executed. Organizational design and change management are also key to successful strategy execution and areas where HR needs to provide expertise.

IT tools can provide the ability to track and model the company's talent pool in ways that give HR compelling data about whether the human capital of the firm is adequate to enact a strategy, where talent is, and how it might be redeployed in order to carry out a strategy. IT tools also can be useful for ongoing sensing of employee reactions to changes that are being implemented and for communication and solicitation of reaction to changes. Electronic HR systems can enable two-way communication with employees to help accelerate learning in the organization and, consequently, the implementation of fundamental changes. Again, however, the ability to use IT for these purposes depends on access to IT expertise in the HR domain.

Current Use of IT

Electronic enabling of HR is well under way. Research suggests that particularly in large organizations, it is becoming a very common practice for many HR transactions.[3] For example, benefits coverage changes, address changes, job posting, and job applications are frequently handled by an e-HR system that has an easy-to-use portal. There are a number of advantages to this, including reduced costs and the opportunity to create a database that can be analyzed for strategic and business partner purposes. Indeed, the process of Web-enabling HR administration is already so well established that the key issue is not whether to do it but how to do it.

The pioneers in creating e-HR systems, perhaps not surprisingly, were technology firms. Sun Microsystems, Dell, Cisco, and Hewlett-Packard, to mention some of the most visible ones, started developing e-HR systems in the mid-1990s. They established relatively sophisticated systems that in some cases went beyond simply doing administrative tasks. They gave advice to managers about how to handle particular kinds of problems and became effective communications vehicles with respect to business directions and plans. In many respects, these systems were quite effective. They reduced costs and allowed HR to gather and analyze data that previously they had not had access to. But the cost of developing these systems and the expertise required to operate them has proven to be very large.

Most of the HR functions that developed e-HR systems for their organizations have their own staff of IT personnel because they had trouble getting support from the IT function. They also have found that updating and maintaining their programs is a substantial and costly activity. For example, in 2002, IBM, with more than 300,000 employees, decided to outsource the maintenance and operation of its e-HR system because the long-term development costs were too high and it was not their core competency. Not only did IBM not have it as a core competency, none of the firms that developed their own systems had HR systems and software as a core competency. These companies created their own systems essentially because no vendor had this expertise, and in order to have a system they had to develop it themselves.

One alternative to developing an e-HR system internally is for an organization to buy a number of process-specific software applications (for example, for compensation and applicant tracking) and combine them to produce an e-HR system. Another alternative is to buy an e-HR system from an ERP vendor such as SAP or PeopleSoft.

HR Outsourcing

Today there are a number of organizations that offer HR BPO services; they handle all of the HR administrative activities, managing an organization's call center, its self-service e-HR systems, and its HRIS system. Outsourcing HR administration is the alternative that we explore in depth in the rest of this book.

In many ways, the HR BPO approach represents the most radical change in how HR services are delivered. It is also the one that potentially can yield the greatest gains for a company. More than any of the other alternatives, if it can be effectively executed, it can free up the HR organization to be a business partner, and it can bring expertise in HR administration that is likely to be available only from a firm that has HR administration as its core competency.

Dealing with multiple companies can provide a BPO firm with a unique opportunity to learn about and develop its technology and HR processes. It can adopt the best practices from its customers and make them its own. It also can try out multiple processes and see which ones work best. It offers the greatest chance of achieving economies of scale since a single outsourcer can service millions of employees. Finally, it offers organizations the greatest degree of scale flexibility when it comes to changes in the size of employee populations. When organizations change the number of people they employ, all they have to do is tell their vendor to change their level of service. They do not have to change the size of their HR function.

Outsourcing certain functions within HR, or in any other department for that matter, is not news by any means. IT providers, for example, have an established record as vendors providing a service to HR departments, and, as we mentioned in Chapter Two, so do benefits administrators, executive search firms, relocation analysts, corporate trainers, corporate coaches, payroll providers, and others.

Limited, focused forays into outsourcing may not free up the HR department so that it can become a high-value-added strategic partner. Outsourcing a single task to a single vendor—say, payroll to a payroll provider—might lower costs to some extent, but it does not go very far toward reducing the number of administrative responsibilities shouldered by the HR executive. The payroll no longer needs tending, so the number of HR staff can be reduced. But the vendor relationship does need attention, and someone also has to manage the interfaces between activities. All of that takes skilled and focused resources. Costs might continue to decrease incrementally, but the time that senior managers must spend tending to the vendors increases. HR executives working with several outsourcing vendors at one time may have limited time to become coaches, facilitators, or architects because their day-to-day operational responsibilities have merely shifted, not disappeared. The management time and attention spent on administration, in other words, remain high because vendors need to be managed and their activities and data integrated.

BPO providers offer a different value proposition. In this approach, HR departments contract with a single provider who handles multiple HR processes and guarantees cost reductions. The HR department need make only an outsourcing connection with a single firm. The outsourcer takes responsibility for virtually all of the administrative tasks of the department that were previously handled internally or by a myriad of individual vendors. HR BPO firms either provide all services themselves or outsource some of the tasks they take on. When they use other vendors, they handle the management of those vendor relationships and act in a service integrator capacity.

The best HR BPO solution ensures that HR work on any one HR process is related to work in the other HR processes. For example, in hiring, HR systems need to identify the skills required for certain jobs and then use these skills in sourcing and screening talent as well as for planning, training and development, compensation, and job assignments. Integrated solutions require vendors with expertise in multiple areas, not single HR practice areas.

In conclusion, HR BPO appears to be a way for an HR department to transform itself into a unit that adds significant strategic value to its organization. In order to do this, however, it must provide an effective and affordable means to exit the HR transaction business, provide integrated HR process, and provide data that help HR become a strategic partner.

The Providers' Landscape

Some companies in the HR outsourcing field are primarily consultants, helping client companies understand how their processes are supposed to work in an outsourcing arrangement and advising them as they select vendors and manage the change process. Others are primarily IT-focused providers, offering software solutions that they either run themselves or sell to the client company. Some are specialists in one or another HR process or straightforward sales-only software vendors. And a few (though we expect the numbers to increase) are dedicated to the concept of being what Lisa Stone, vice president and director of research at the Gartner Group, an industry analyst, calls "pure-play" BPO providers.

The HR BPO players have emerged (and are still cropping up) from a variety of places. Some companies, like ACS, EDS, and Accenture, moved into BPO from specializations in IT outsourcing. Some, like Fidelity and Hewitt, had existing strongholds as consultants, systems builders, or financial service providers. Still others, like Convergys, are established providers of customer transaction services, such as billing. Fidelity has branched into other HR outsourcing areas from its position as an administrator of retirement accounts. Irvine, California–based Exult was created for the sole purpose of providing HR BPO on the strength of an entrepreneurial vision of how HR departments will be evolving over the next generation.

The competitive landscape for providers is taking shape along the lines of client size and also along a spectrum of complexity that ranges from processing a single type of transaction to full-scale process transformation in the HR function. As the market matures, the landscape is likely to change substantially.

Data support the notion that HR BPO companies have broken ground in a growth market. According to the Gartner Group, HR administrative tasks topped the list of processes outsourced in 2003 and will remain there for some time.

Gartner data also indicate that by 2007, HR BPO will be a $37.8 billion-plus industry, up from $25 billion in 2002, for an 8.6 percent annual growth rate. BPO in general will be a $173.5 billion industry by 2007, up from $110 billion in 2002, according to Gartner.[4] Much of the growth is taking place in North America, but western Europe is also seeing significant increases in the HR BPO market, with slower but steady growth predicted in the much smaller and less mature markets for HR BPO in the Asia-Pacific region, Japan, and Latin America.

Just as demand is growing, supply is growing too. The HR BPO market is experiencing high levels of competition among first-mover companies, at a time when the business model for HR BPO firms is still evolving. Key questions that remain to be answered include how profitable this business will be, how many companies can survive in this space, and what the most effective business models are.

First Mover: Exult

In 1999 Exult became the first company to sign a major HR BPO contract. In 2003, it operated at a profit with more than a dozen Global 500 clients engaged in long-term contracts totaling over $4 billion. The company is one of the few pure-play, or service integrator, BPO providers. It offers what its senior managers internally refer to as the "full multi," that is, a value proposition that offers to take on all of a client's HR administrative work and run it, along with other client work, from a number of call center and administrative hubs, on a multiclient, multicenter, multishore, multishift basis.

In 2003, the company acquired PriceWaterhouseCoopers' international BPO business operations (reflected in the figures just noted), an act that substantially expanded its geographical coverage outside the United States to include multiprocess service centers in South America and the United Kingdom, along with a presence in eastern Europe, western Europe, Hong Kong, and Singapore.

At the beginning of 2004, Exult was providing a variety of HR–related services to approximately 500,000 employees; it was managing more than $21 billion per year in payroll and more than $35 billion per year in accounts payable. In June, Hewitt and Exult announced a merger that will create a company with over twenty HR BPO clients.

We will examine Exult in depth because it is a useful case study, particularly for HR managers considering a BPO arrangement. Exult was the first HR BPO provider to offer comprehensive HR administration for multiple clients. Thus, we can examine how HR BPO works in multiple companies. In addition, because its customer relationships are mature, it is possible to see how HR BPO works once it has become a standard way of doing HR in a company.

Notes

1. Lawler, E. E., III, and Mohrman, S. A. (2003). *Creating a Strategic Human Resources Organization: An Assessment of Trends and New Directions*. Palo Alto, Calif.: Stanford University Press.
2. Lawler, E. E. III, and Mohrman, S. A. (2004). Human resources management: New consulting opportunities. In L. Greiner and F. Poulfelt (eds.), *Handbook of Management Consulting: The Contemporary Consultant*. Cincinnati, Ohio: South-Western.
3. Lawler and Mohrman. (2003).
4. Gartner Dataquest. (July 2003).

Chapter Five

Exult

Exult was not created to be an HR BPO company. Initially, when General Atlantic Partners' Michael Cline (senior partner) and Steve Denning (managing partner) decided to fund the creation of a BPO enterprise, they didn't know that the focus would end up being on HR processes; they just knew that their analyses had revealed that BPO was a field with tremendous potential.

In fact, even when Jim Madden, Exult's CEO, was approached to be the chief executive of the start-up, the company's business focus had yet to be determined. Madden started his career at Andersen Consulting (Accenture), where he sold the firm's first outsourcing contract on the West Coast; from there, he became a principal with Booz-Allen & Hamilton. He joined Systemhouse, a Canadian technology and outsourcing company, in early 1993 as vice president and managing director of its Los Angeles office to help it grow into the U.S. market. At the time he got the call from General Atlantic Partners, he had been with Systemhouse for five years. Progressing from office managing director to president of the U.S. market at Systemhouse, he had become the chief financial officer (and Systemhouse, for its part, had become a $1.7 billion division of MCI).

Madden recalls, "I got a call from Julia Flint, who was, at the time, recruiting for Ramsey-Beirne, to interview for the chief executive position of a BPO company that General Atlantic Partners was going to finance. I was told that GA Partners was going to invest $50 million in some sort of business process outsourcing entity. But even when I first sat down with Michael and Steve, neither of them knew that the focus of the business was going to be human resources."

Madden met first with Michael Cline and, in his words, was "blown away" by the proposal on the table. Tired of running a large division of a public company and intrigued by the thought of running his own show, he joined General Atlantic Partners in 1998. The company then retained McKinsey to help learn what processes executives at Fortune 100 companies were most likely to outsource and which among them represented the best opportunity for BPO to add value and to be profitable for the provider.

HR emerged as the clear leader. As Madden recalls, "We kept talking to CEOs, CFOs, and heads of HR, and they told us time and again that if we could take HR off their hands, we could have it."

The idea was not without its detractors. Early on, the company also sought the advice of several seasoned HR consultants, who almost universally proclaimed the imminent demise of the concept. A variety of reasons were cited, chief among them that "no one would buy the service." But the positive reactions and feedback General Atlantic Partners received from company executives was ultimately more compelling. "The process was actually quick," Madden remembers. "It only took sixty days to pin down what we wanted to do."

Honing a Business Model

The challenge became developing the business model and signing a client. Madden, along with Cline, Denning, and Steve Unterberger (who joined Exult in March 1999 as COO), started with a conceptual model based on the idea that the company would:

- Deliver all transactional and administrative HR services and processes and create for the client a single point of contact and accountability.
- Develop capabilities that would complement and complete best-in-class HR service components, including deep process expertise.

• Apply new tools and technologies to standardize and improve services, implementing best-practice information and technology across processes to create more streamlined processes and reduce costs.

• Operate multiclient, commercial, and professional manufacturing-oriented processing centers; that is, focus on serving multiple external customers rather than setting up or running shared-service operations for individual clients at client locales, and run the processes with the metrics and disciplines of a manufacturing company: measuring inputs, outputs, throughputs, and quality. Importantly, the company's call centers would not be one-off centers for each client because that approach would not lend itself to efficiency through scale. It would not leverage processes, management, and technology. Instead, each call center would process work for multiple clients, and a single client's work might be spread over several Exult processing centers in the interest of using the centers fully and getting the scale necessary to reduce costs.

• Manage the flow of HR transaction information (including information from third-party vendors) from a central vantage point, offering the client's managers and employees a single point of contact for comprehensive, integrated, and flexible HR services.

• Be accountable not only for services provided directly but also for the performance of the entire network of providers.

• Source third-party vendors strategically to reduce costs and improve service levels for clients by negotiating aggregate spend discounts and seasoned contract management principles.

• Forge new working relationships with the client's existing vendors or recommend new best-of-class providers, thus rationalizing the client's formal contractual partnerships.

• Apply performance-based metrics to all activities based on mutual goals set and agreed on by Exult and its clients.

The founders knew that in order for their model to yield truly breakthrough results, three fundamental objectives would have to be achieved. First, the client's HR managers would have to partner with Exult's managers to reengineer internal processes with an eye toward aligning HR as a true strategic partner in the client business. Many companies that have attempted to achieve such transformation through traditional outsourcing contracts have failed to meet their goals because traditional, incremental outsourcing looks only at single processes. In doing so, it misses the wholesale gains needed across all HR processes to unshackle the HR organization and enable it to take a more strategic role.

Second, Exult would have to learn the client's markets, including any cultural and regulatory factors associated with foreign operations.

Third, Exult would have to offer sustainable world-class solutions, continuous improvement, value generation, and a customer-oriented service approach. Once the partnership between client and provider was established, Exult would have to keep abreast of changes in the client's company so that it would be ready to expand or contract its operations as needed to handle growth and downsizing seamlessly. Exult would also have to be current with respect to any client technology changes that might affect HR processes.

The second and third expectations set high performance bars but were straightforward. The first, however, was something Madden and his backers recognized as a critical gamble. Consider the implications of the word *partner*. The idea was not that Exult would work "for" a client but that it would "partner" with the client on a path to realign HR as a true strategic contributor.

The idea relied heavily on the expectation that HR professionals would be concerned not only with reducing costs but also with transforming their function. If successful, this new kind of BPO-client relationship would align the commercial interests of both parties to create a relationship based on mutual gain. It would also enable both parties to assess performance regularly and adopt changes as needed.

As Madden puts it, "No company is going to approach us without a significant expectation regarding cost reduction. Cost reduction is always going to be a driver in this business. But ultimately, the work is about value added on an ongoing basis, and this requires the provider to be an extension of the client."

Rob Galford, managing partner at the Center for Executive Development in Boston, likes to ask business leaders who are considering any sort of organizational transformation to "think about what's on their plate." Often, at executive development classes, he passes out actual paper plates and asks all those in the class to map their existing responsibilities, allotting space according to demands on their time (not according to relative importance). Then he passes out another round of plates and asks the students to map their time as they would like to see it used. The contrast between the first and second "plates" is often illuminating, and sometimes it even suggests immediate paths to greater job satisfaction and contribution.

What Madden and his colleagues planned to offer clients was their take on the "second plate"—their view, in other words, of how an HR department might be able to focus its energies if it engaged in a relationship with an HR BPO provider that took responsibility for HR administration. Figure 5.1 illustrates what was, and remains, Exult's aspirations for the ideal provider-client scenario.

"We like to think of Exult as being the engine room of its clients," Madden says. "We are the power behind them, allowing them to chart the course, adjust the course, and focus on the destination rather than on the details of how the engine works."

The Economics

Exult's value proposition called for the company to guarantee its clients an agreed-on cost reduction on a significant portion of the processes under contract (primarily those that are labor based). Other processes would be gain-shared between the client and the provider—that is, as savings were achieved, they would be split between Exult and the client. Exult would put its capital to work and at risk so that the client could allocate capital to the core, strategic

Figure 5.1 The Exult Business Model for HR BPO

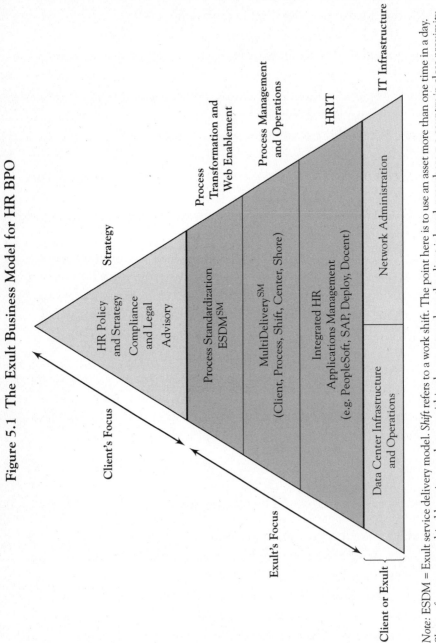

Note: ESDM = Exult service delivery model. *Shift* refers to a work shift. The point here is to use an asset more than one time in a day. *Shore* refers to geographical location: onshore = within the country where the client is based; near shore = a country in close proximity with relatively lower costs; offshore = work performed in a very low-cost country.

activities of its business. Exult would receive a rate of return measured by overall gross margins that would be commensurate with the risk and the work performed.

Madden and the company's backers knew that Exult's internal business model would have to evolve as the company grew. Initially, they planned to grow through acquisition: they would hire the bulk of their first clients' HR staffs. These people, newly acquired Exult employees, would first run processes for their former employers as they always had, but over time they would use the systems and programs Exult preferred and serve other customers as well.

The plan was that as Exult signed on more clients, it would stop hiring client staff in bulk and instead would bring on only a few key people from each new client company. Exult's existing staff would absorb the work of the new client, filling capacity gradually at each processing center and reducing the cost of processing work for each client. Ultimately Exult would achieve the volume needed to be a highly profitable entity.

Financial success for Exult would mean delivering real profits, defined to be operating margins in the teens. Furthermore, the profits would have to be delivered without any sleight of hand for off-balance-sheet, special-purpose entities. To address that issue head-on, Madden and his colleagues determined and applied the most conservative accounting processes used by any outsourcer. (Admittedly, they knew that that conservative approach would initially have a negative impact on profits, as it would have the perverse effect of increasing losses with increasing sales until the company reached critical mass.)

Financial success would depend on market share and the size of the market. To gain access to capital, Exult had to show profit potential and convince investors that the market was scalable and would lead to substantial revenues and growth opportunities. Return on capital and equity would be a critical measure. Exult's model aimed to demonstrate return on equity of over 30 percent and approaching 50 percent, substantially more than IT outsourcing.

Finally, as Madden says, "We knew that at the end of the day, cash would be king. Positive free cash flow and cash flow from operations would be important long-term measures in the business as it grew to scale."

Starting Up, Gaining Scale

The four chapters that follow detail case studies of Exult clients. Chapter Six, which focuses on Exult's first customer, BP, serves the dual purpose of illustrating both BP's venture into HR BPO and Exult's experience in attracting and working with this first client. In the remainder of this chapter, we highlight a few of the key milestones of Exult's development that illustrate how, over the past four years, the company has gained scale and put into operation its business model:

• In November 1999, Exult purchased the consulting firm Gunn Partners, which was already engaged with Exult working on client development. Gunn Partners made its mark in the early 1990s through consulting work to the Fortune 500 on shared service centers. Madden was introduced to Bob Gunn through a research associate at General Atlantic Partners who was searching on behalf of the company to find an HR process consultancy that had strong operating and benchmarking metrics. Exult was already in talks with BP when Gunn came on the scene. With just thirty employees, Exult lacked the critical mass it needed to move to the next stage with BP. Madden and Gunn reached the agreement to have Exult acquire Gunn Partners in October 1999; the final negotiations of the deal were worked out in London while the parties were negotiating the BP contract. Exult signed its first client contract, with BP, in December 1999.

• Shortly after signing BP as a client, Exult signed a contract with a very different company, Tenneco (before its corporate split-up), to establish a processing center in Houston with more than eighty employees. This contract was a critical factor in enabling Exult to do work for BP in the United States.

• During 1999, Exult began the process of establishing a board of directors. If the company was going to have clients with the size and stature of BP, it was critically important to have a board that would add value and provide good governance. General Atlantic Partners introduced Madden to Tom Neff, chairman of Spencer Stuart U.S., a global executive recruiting firm, and Mike Spence, then dean of the Stanford Graduate School of Business. After meeting with Madden, both Neff and Spence agreed to join the board. (Subsequently, Spence received the Nobel Prize in Economic Sciences, and Neff was listed as one of Fortune's "50 most influential people.") In addition, Neff helped Madden recruit Mike Miles, the former chairman of Phillip Morris, as a board member. Madden also recruited a long-time mentor from Systemhouse, John Oltman, Systemhouse's chairman, and the former partner in charge of Accenture (Andersen Consulting) for the United States.

• Early in 2000, with the BP contract in place, Exult was approached by numerous investment bankers who wanted to lead an initial public offering (IPO). The IPO was successfully completed in the second quarter of 2000; the deal priced at $10 a share and implied a market value of about $1 billion.

• In August 2000, Exult signed a seven-year $200 million contract with Unisys for comprehensive HR administration.

• In November 2000, the company signed a ten-year, $1.1 billion contract with Bank of America, providing payroll and benefits administration, recruiting and employee contact services, HRIS/ application services management, accounts payable, travel and expenses administration, relocation services, and expatriate administration to some 143,000 Bank of America employees. This contract also involved the acquisition of a service center with 550 employees in Charlotte, North Carolina. (Bank of America is the subject of Chapter Seven.)

• A contract with International Paper was signed in the fourth quarter of 2001 and one with Prudential in the first quarter of 2002. The International Paper contract included the acquisition of a service center in Memphis with about 150 employees. The case study regarding its experience with BPO is chronicled in Chapter Eight, and Prudential's experience is reported in Chapter Nine.

- Early in 2001, Exult recognized the need to move some work offshore. Scouting teams of managers explored various locales, including Ireland, eastern Europe, and India. Exult decided on India based on cost, the quality of the available workforce, and the English-language skills of potential employees, among other factors.

The transition of work to India has happened in several phases. Phase One called for Exult to move its IT support offshore to two Indian providers, HCL and Hexaware. Phase Two originally called for the company to secure a local BPO partner, but Exult changed that plan when it could not identify an Indian company that had the requisite skills to do HR BPO. In November 2002, Exult decided to set up its own India-based operations, and in a subsequent board meeting, Madden presented and received approval for a $10 million project to set up a processing center in India. The facility, located in New Mumbai (Bombay), is designed to accommodate approximately five hundred employees. Exult hopes to staff to capacity in 2004. By the end of 2003, the center was successfully processing calls and transactions for clients.

- Exult achieved profitability in the fourth quarter of 2002. It had initially planned to become profitable by mid-2002, based on analyses conducted in 2000. Once it failed to reach that goal, achieving profitability became a major internal motivating factor among company employees in October, November, and December 2002.

- Achieving profitability was not without its challenges. In the summer of 2000, Exult's auditor, Arthur Andersen, collapsed, and the company was forced to change auditors. It selected KPMG, which initially determined that the company's method of accounting was overly conservative. Exult subsequently announced that it would seek to change its accounting to be more in line with outsourcing industry standards, but as Madden recalls, one long-term investor's response to that move was to say, "That's like announcing fire in a crowded movie theater." The stock plummeted from a high of about $12 in 2002 to a low of $1.97 by December 2002. It took achievement of profitability to regain traction and an improved stock price. (The company also had a strong balance sheet, with over $100 million in cash and no debt.)

Internally, Madden reports, the low point did have an upside: very little employee turnover occurred when the stock price dropped, and Exult experienced no client turnover. As he puts it, the "rough spot fostered resilience among managers, employees and clients."

• Over the course of 2003, the company gained momentum, first signing a $500 million, ten-year contract with the Bank of Montreal (which involved the opening of a service center in Toronto). Exult also signed contracts with Circuit City, Universal Music Group, Vivendi Universal Entertainment, and McKesson, and it embarked on an initiative to implement the principles of Six Sigma throughout its operations.

A critical transaction in 2003 was Exult's acquisition of PriceWaterhouseCoopers' (PwC) international BPO business for $17 million. The purchase gave Exult a substantially expanded global footprint (four continents), added a non-English-language capability, and a trained employee base of over five hundred. The purchase also included client BPO contracts with remaining terms of two to six years and an aggregate revenue run rate of approximately $25 million per year. Some of these contracts included non-HR processes. The clients included Standard Chartered Bank, Equifax (United Kingdom), Safeway (United Kingdom), Tibbet & Britten, and Grupo Algar. The PwC acquisition advanced the globalization of Exult and signaled that as HRO providers gain proficiency in handling HR administration, other functions can be folded into the mix.

As Kevin Campbell (Exult's COO) told reporter Jay Whitehead of *HRO Today*, in an interview published in the July–August 2003 issue, "The facts are, aspects of F&A, such as payroll, are 50% HR and 50% finance. When you ask if that function is HR or finance, a lot of people would say 'both.' So for some time, we have been doing both. If you're already handling people's paychecks, it's an easy step, for example, to include travel expenses. So why not include it in our services? This is just a natural extension of services. Our past deals with clients such as Bank of America, Universal, and Prudential have all included fixed assets and general accounting aspects. People put together deals where they are. For HR, that trend includes payroll, and some companies would go so far as to consider that it includes all of F&A." In that spirit, Exult today calls itself an HR-led BPO rather than an HR BPO.

Business Model Evolution

In early 2004, Exult had offices in California and London, with client service centers in Texas, Tennessee, North Carolina, Ontario, Glasgow, Rotterdam, and Mumbai, India. The company's top managers are increasingly thinking of centers that are specialized by process; for example, most of Exult's accounts payable services are run out of the Charlotte center, as are the company's call centers. Fulfillment is increasingly run out of Memphis. Learning and global mobility services are run exclusively out of the Houston office.

As the company's American president, Mike Salvino, explains,

We do processes that are very transactional-intensive, and then we do other processes that are more high touch. For example, relocation services—expatriate or otherwise—are more high touch. At any given time, BP, for example, has maybe 3,000 people in expatriate mode and maybe 250 folks from the Bank of America relocating. Payroll, on the other hand, is transaction intensive. So you might see us evolving along the lines of having a huge transactional hub like our Charlotte facility, in which we just crank, crank, crank payroll, and crank accounts payable, and having another hub, as we do in Houston, that does more of the high-touch work.

Recruiting is another story. We have thirty-seven offices across the United States working on recruiting activity because of the nature of the work. We can't run recruiting effectively out of one center because when you're recruiting midlevel managers and below, you really want and need to be able to have a presence in that market to get the job done right.

As Exult matures, the company will likely adjust its operations further to reflect the ways in which it can best achieve economies of scale and deliver those savings to clients. Currently, Exult is different things to different clients. The company neither requires clients to adopt a set of standardized processes immediately nor does it offer to work entirely with the processes and systems a client is already using.

Exult does not impose on clients a set of standard practices that it has found to be superior, nor does it simply operate the existing client setup. Instead, it takes the position that there *is* no uniform model or approach that will work equally well for all large public companies. Every company has a mix of existing processes—some efficient and effective, some one or the other, some neither. Every company also has existing policies regarding HR administration—some good, some possibly more complex than they need to be. And every company has its own way of doing things, which also might be more (or less) efficient, effective, and user friendly. The goal is to improve performance continually across those areas in a way that makes sense for the company at hand. "Best practice" is a term Exult managers use sparingly, if ever; company executives stress that they are more concerned with identifying areas of potential improvement and understanding the levers that drive improvement in each case.

Exult has established partnerships with an array of vendors. That group includes Ceridian for EAP as well as resource and referral consultation services; Deloitte & Touche for expatriate software; Deploy Solutions for Web-enabled staffing; Docent for Web-enabled training administration; HCL Technologies for offshore IT services and product engineering; Hexaware Technologies for offshore software services; IQ Navigator for vendor-neutral sourcing for temp staff; Lee Hecht Harrison for outplacement services; ReloAction for employee relocation services; Skills Soft for e-learning; and Towers Perrin for health and welfare administration services.

There are often compelling financial reasons to use vendors from Exult's stable, but the company does not require clients to sign on with its preferred vendors from the start or even commit to using them thereafter. With regard to software, for example, Exult supports and favors SAP or PeopleSoft applications. But the software decision isn't as important as moving clients to one consolidated platform (often from a fragmented state). Thus far, Exult has converted its clients to either SAP or PeopleSoft. The economies of scale Exult needs have compelled the conversions.

"We stop short of saying that we won't support anything other than SAP or PeopleSoft," Kevin Campbell says. "But in almost all cases, the financial case is so much better with our tools that we get clients to use our tools if not on day one, then over time."

The same is true with services. In the early days of the company, Exult did not have preferred partners. Today it does, so Exult executives try to make an economic case with new clients to use those partners. Most of the time, clients agree. As Campbell says, "If they have a concern, then we review the service and savings opportunities. To date, we don't say 'our way or the highway,' but we have been very successful at demonstrating why our partners work and what the synergies and savings can be from using them."

As Exult looks at its clients' operations from the inside out, it asks the following questions:

- What are the existing policies? What should be getting done? What is getting done? Are the existing policies actually limiting the delivery of services?

- What are the existing processes? How are things getting done? Are existing processes building in errors that need to be exposed and dealt with at a root-cause level?

- What are the existing inputs and outputs? What are the employees, or users, seeing? What interface are they used to? What kinds of data are they used to supplying? What kind of information are they used to receiving? In what form? How frequently?

- How are the operations currently being run? What works, and what doesn't? What kind of information is being generated through existing policies? What kind could be generated? What kind of knowledge could come out of doing things a different way?

Company expectations regarding the use of the Web are also weighed heavily. Exult has become (by design and by necessity) a Web-enabled company. Putting existing HR processes on the Web for client employees to access directly in order to engage in self-service, and using data mining skills to provide new HR-related services on the Web is a priority. The services Exult can provide run the gamut from basic policy and reference material, to employee self-service and manager self-service. Exult can also provide data indexes on employee satisfaction and drivers of success. (The case studies in the chapters that follow explore HR on the Web in more detail.) Exult managers are careful to temper expectations for HR on the Web based on their customers' readiness to make the move.

Conclusion

Exult's long-term success depends on its ability to deliver on the promise of efficiencies of scale and its ability to deliver measurable process improvement. Its merger with Hewitt Associates promises to improve its offerings. The merged company will have greater scale and be able to take advantage of Hewitt's process and content expertise in compensation and benefits. It will be capable of offering total HR BPO services on an integrated basis with HR consulting expertise.

Exult remains committed to a client-provider partnership as a cornerstone of its approach. Improvements on the client side of things are a necessary part of Exult's own ability to deliver. Exult also shares an expectation with its clients that in improving the performance of transactional activities, the two parties will gain increased identification of and access to meaningful metrics. Exult expects that these metrics will foster improved performance in the day-to-day administration of HR and the transformation of the HR function overall into a strategic player. That may prove to be an important competitive advantage as the industry unfolds.[1]

Note

1. For another view of Exult, see Adler, P. (2003). Making the HR outsourcing decision. *MIT Sloan Management Review*, 45(1):5, 3–60.

Chapter Six

BP

Business: Oil and gas

Contract signing: Fourth quarter 1999

Contract term: Initial seven-year relationship framework

Contract value: Initially $600 million, plus Arco, Burmah Castrol add-ons

Geographical coverage: United States and United Kingdom

Employees in company: Approximately 100,000 at contract signing

Employees covered: 56,000

Scope: Payroll, benefits administration, compensation administration, recruiting, expatriate administration, relocation, employee contact, HRIS/ASM, training administration, vendor management, compliance reporting, and severance processing

The BP case is valuable on several fronts. First, it illustrates the difficulties of moving through uncharted territory in the areas of HR BPO and e-HR. Second, it illuminates the way a well-respected company approached the prospect of outsourcing HR processes and putting HR "on the Web." Third, it provides hard-learned lessons for companies that are considering HR BPO. Finally, it provides an interesting piece of business history in tumultuous times, as it chronicles the case of a start-up company working with its first customer in a make-or-break deal.

This case is best considered in four parts: (1) BP's actions regarding HR outsourcing before Exult came on the scene, (2) the period during which BP and Exult negotiated their contract, (3) the initial transition phase, and (4) operations post-transition.

Considering HR Outsourcing

The topic of HR outsourcing had been of interest to top HR executives at BP for some time, but they had never formally taken steps to explore whether HR BPO was right for them and whether there were vendors available to handle the administrative work they might want to outsource. But by 1997, outsourcing at least some administrative tasks seemed to be an imperative. HR managers were immersed in the day-to-day details of running HR administration for an extremely large, complex organization, and they were swamped with paperwork. They could see a clear need for HR to contribute to the company in a much more strategic way, but in order to do it, they needed to free themselves up to gather and leverage the information and expertise they had. They envisioned an HR department that could harness the vast knowledge and expertise present in the organization and deploy it where it was most needed at any given time.

There had been talk in the past and several internal studies about what kinds of HR processes could be comprehensively outsourced, how outsourcing could be accomplished, and the potential upsides and downsides. A few initiatives had been launched, but none with staying power. Now there was a new sense of urgency, for several reasons.

First, oil prices were low, so cost reduction was a priority. BP executives the world over were charged with streamlining operations and tightening belts.

Second, BP in Europe (what the company internally refers to as Heritage BP) already had experience with several successful outsourcing ventures. The company had outsourced its UK upstream accounting services at the start of the 1990s to Andersen Consulting followed by downstream accounting across Europe to both Andersen and Price Waterhouse. Outsourcing IT activities and facilities management, primarily in the United States and United Kingdom, followed. A reservoir of experience and outsource service management skill was available, and it provided evidence of performance improvement benefits from outsourcing.

Third, the company seemed to be developing the scale it needed to make outsourcing HR administrative processes worth the effort. It was merging with Amoco (declared in August 1998 and ratified at year end). A merger with Arco, announced in April 1999 and ratified in April 2000, followed soon after. Each company was a significant player in the energy business, but all were market followers, overshadowed by the market leaders Exxon and Shell. The new company was an oil industry leader and one of the ten largest business entities in the world, with over 100,000 employees.

Finally, the merger activity had created something of a "burning bridge:" BP had an evolving roster of different HR processes to reconcile, even if it didn't turn to outsourcing as a solution.

As one BP manager says, looking back, "There was so much overlap in processes because of the mergers; it was the perfect time to think about tackling the new and different. BP had always made decluttering a priority. Decluttering, in fact, is one way to think about BP's business model. The idea is that management folks anywhere in the organization should be able to focus on the most important parts of their business—the most strategically critical components of their jobs. In order to do that, they should be able to let other things go."

As BP HR executive Peter Whalley, who has been involved in the process from the earliest days, now says, "As we looked at what BP was evolving into—the size of the organization, its strengths, its vulnerable spots—we were constantly asking: 'Which cultures among the newly merged companies in the human resources area—and in other areas as well—were most desirable? How were decisions being made in different companies, in different functions, in different geographies? Which were the most effective? Which would be most effective over the long term in a larger organizational context?' The current model was out of options, and the time was ripe to ask questions about the best practices to use going forward."

Untested Territory

The time was ripe, but HR BPO was untested territory. If BP truly wanted to outsource a large number of HR processes to a single provider, it would be breaking new ground, and whatever provider it contracted with would be breaking new ground as well. That concept, however, didn't seem to faze BP managers. As Whalley points out (and he is echoed almost verbatim by several other senior-level managers in the organization), "BP is in the business of taking risks. We're digging holes in the ground, looking for oil. There aren't many businesses riskier than that to begin with. So pursuing an outsourcing arrangement with no trailblazer ahead really wasn't a concern." What was needed was a group of BP managers to spearhead the effort and turn the talk into something tangible.

Don Packham was one of the critical members of that early team. For Packham, the journey toward outsourcing HR processes had begun in 1993 when he was working in London, responsible for HR in the upstream business. (BP is organized almost entirely by business line. The main businesses are upstream activities: finding, producing, and shipping crude oil. Downstream activities include fuels and lubricants refining, distribution, and marketing; gas, power, and renewables: gas supply and sales, power generation, and photovoltaic (solar) panel manufacture and sales; and petrochemicals—the manufacture and marketing of oil-based chemical products.) Packham had long been mulling over how technology could help the HR function become more efficient, and more effective. And to that end, he had several meetings with people from the London office of Accenture (formerly Andersen Consulting), which had been thinking about what outsourcing it could offer for the HR function.

"We understood each other," Packham remembers. "There were great thoughts on the table and a promising vision. They could see what I was talking about. But they weren't ready, and neither were we, really. So nothing came of it. But we didn't discard the idea; we just put it on the back burner."

Then in 1994, Packham agreed to sponsor some work around the process of expatriation. This is a critical process for BP, which regularly moves promising managers into new and increasingly challenging jobs as part of their personal growth plans. Was the process something that could be handled properly by a vendor, and was it even possible given the number of providers involved? Expatriation involves, among other things, moving companies, tax advisers, host services companies, and government agency coordinators. Was there anyone who could integrate all of that seamlessly?

KPMG was starting to enter the business process outsourcing market; it was the successful bidder in an early round of proposals for BP's expatriate business. But as Packham and his colleague Hilary Ware, then U.S. HR services leader, were working to structure a deal, word came down from the top managers at BP that they would not approve the transaction. Expatriates were very important, and even for a company that welcomed risk taking, this proposition was *too* risky.

Again, the company didn't go forward with outsourcing. But again, Packham's investment in the project wasn't wasted. He and his fellow BP managers were learning about the potential and the limits of outsourcing business processes. It was a matter of matching the right processes with the right company, at the right time.

Several years later, in 1996, BP entered into an agreement to form a joint venture with Mobil across Europe. As Packham says, "Suddenly, we had two of everything, in terms of the HR function, in each country. So we started to think, 'What if we could find an outsourcer that could create a pan-European solution for HR administrative processes?'" Packham by that time was also responsible for the group HR center in London and agreed to be part of the team of people who would explore the options.

At that point, Nick Starritt entered the picture. Starritt, who joined BP from Mobil and had a background in HR as well as experience with outsourcing accounting activities, was named HR director in the Global Business Center in late 1997. His mandate was to lead the so-called Project for a Pan-European Solution, at the same time considering possibilities for a vehicle that could handle U.S. HR administration as well.

Starritt, along with Packham, Ware, Howard Nelson, and two other colleagues, worked steadily through 1997 appraising the market, and in early 1998 they selected Price Waterhouse (now PwC) for joint development of an HR BPO model with the prospect of PwC providing the services.

Then in August 1998, BP announced merger intentions with Amoco. Packham recalls, "Nick and I said to ourselves, 'This might be just the platform that allows us to go ahead and create a BP/PwC company to run all of the transactional processes for both of us. And it might work in other parts of the world as well.'"

A deal seemed possible. A letter of intent to move into detailed contract negotiations was prepared in autumn 1998, but it was never approved. In the following few months, it became apparent that the parties were not aligned in their objectives, and ultimately the initiative broke down. Packham, who had moved to Chicago to work on the integration of BP and Amoco in addition to exploring the possible joint venture with PwC, found that PwC's partners were increasingly wary. "They couldn't see how they could make money in the business," he remembers. Whalley concurs: "As a result of their own merger, their commitment toward this new line of outsourcing shifted, as did the way in which they were interested in doing a deal with us. And we concluded eventually that a partnership organization was not the type of corporate vehicle that could tolerate the risk sharing we sought in this innovative endeavor. By March 1999, we were at the breakdown point with them."

"Some people didn't want to let go," Whalley remembers. "Some people were saying, 'We've invested all this time; let's cut a deal on their terms and make the best of it.' It was hard to disengage mentally from something we had come so close to make happen. But we had to. The fit was no longer there."

Whalley credits Starritt with keeping BP true to its intent as the PwC deal broke down. As he says, "In order for an initiative of this nature to work, it needs a critical piece of leadership holding constant to the intent. Nick provided that leadership. He was the person who kept everyone in the circle, even when there were people trying to charge out of it in all directions."

Acceptable Risk

Once again, a potential contract had fallen through. But this time, BP remained committed to the idea of outsourcing HR administration. Nick Starritt agreed with Don Packham that the initiative should not be put on hold and that the company should take another look at vendors. The BPO landscape had indeed changed. A host of companies now seemed to be on the verge of offering the kinds of services BP was seeking. This time, the company tried not to let the momentum of its effort die.

During the course of its talks with Price Waterhouse, BP had completed several risk analysis workshops. The company now turned to the results of these workshops as it began to search for a provider that could fit the bill. In the workshops, BP brought together a group of people from diverse backgrounds within the company, all of whom had experience with new ventures. Given the proposition of outsourcing HR administrative duties, they brainstormed the sorts of issues that would need to be dealt with. They first assembled into groups along functional lines—for example, financial people in a group, and audit and control specialists, lawyers, and line managers in another. Then they looked at the issues from the point of manageability. What would an outsourcing arrangement do to internal control? Was there a substantive market–driven risk? The groups then considered if the risks they had identified could be managed. Finally, they all reported their results. And as Packham says, "We started to see a pattern of whether those risks— associated with each solution—were tolerable."

BP determined that the right partner should be willing to take the risk to the same extent that BP itself was willing to take on the risk. "We realized that we wanted the outsourcer's skin in the game as much as our own and on the same time line," says Whalley. "Put another way, we were prepared to be a guinea pig in the field of BPO so long as the other party was also going to be a guinea pig and suffer the same things we would suffer. We knew we needed a partner that understood what needed to happen and that had adequate dedicated funds. Experience wouldn't necessarily matter, as this was a new sort of venture entirely. We wanted a partner that would assure us that our success would be their success in this deal."

The Start-Up

It was in January 1999 that Hilary Ware suggested that Don Packham meet Michael Cline and Steve Denning, the senior partner and the managing partner, respectively, of General Atlantic Partners. When Packham met Cline and Denning in Houston, the two venture capitalists told him that they were putting money into the HR area and that they had identified, in particular, HR business process outsourcing. And as Packham recalls, "Cline said, 'I know exactly what you're trying to do. We've hired a guy name Jim Madden to create a business to fill that exact need. We're going to support him to do this; we'd like you to meet with Jim.'"

Within a month, Packham and Ware had their initial meeting with Madden. Packham now says that he knew in that first meeting that they had found what they were looking for. "He described his vision of a BPO company for HR processes. Our vision overlapped almost identically. What Jim was talking about building was exactly what we had been seeking."

Exult was running against others at this point in the vendor selection process, but when BP again ran a series of risk analysis workshops, this time with a well-financed start-up organization plugged in as the partner, the results showed risks that were manageable. "We saw that we wouldn't just be dependent on the provider; we saw that we wouldn't just be dependent on external market forces. We knew that in this kind of a deal, we could take action ourselves to deal with any issues that arose," Packham says. The BP leaders concluded that a company that didn't yet exist might in fact be preferable to one that already had a track record as an outsourcer in areas other than HR.

Exult went through a formal bidding process between March and June 1999 and a subsequent due diligence process, which lasted three more months. During that time, Exult gained insight into the fragmented state and volume of HR processes at BP, and BP checked Exult's foundation and backers. Contract negotiations extended over six months, and the contract was signed at the end of December 1999. The results of the due diligence process were clearly favorable, and in the course of service contract negotiation, a parallel agreement was struck for BP to take a limited ownership stake in Exult to help align its interests with the economic success of Exult and its growth.

There were other significant positive signs for Exult as well. BP supported Exult's plan to expand its client roster as quickly as possible, even as it was starting its work with BP. In fact, one of BP's requirements was that whatever the company did with regard to outsourcing HR activities had to have commercial possibilities. "We didn't want something that was always going to be unique to BP," Whalley says. "Our initial business model of what a BPO arrangement would look like called for commercialization to be a part of it in order to keep the service offering at a leading-edge, innovative level.

"It's not our business to be chasing the best tools in the marketplace," Whalley explains. "What we were interested in—what we're still interested in—is, 'Do the results of that work allow us to conduct our business in market-leading form?'"

In other words, BP wanted the market forces to ensure that Exult remains at the top of its game. "If Exult's only client were BP, we could get locked into a certain way of doing things," says Whalley. "Over time in that situation, what would be the point of outsourcing? But if Exult had other clients, it would keep the organization updating in order to stay competitive, looking at best in market."

Whalley explains the logic in greater detail:

The recruiting process provides an example of the importance of a provider that is bound to stay current with best practice tools. If you take a list of two thousand applications for a job, the process of culling to get the list down to thirty people is fairly standard. The filters that are set up in terms of the criteria that identify and attract the best people for your particular organization are up to you [the client]. But the process is up to the BPO provider. What's important to the "client" company is not the process used to get to the final thirty candidates in the short list. It is the quality of candidates in that final list and whether the people the client ultimately hires are great fits. What's important is the outcome. *How* the client uses the tool is more important than which tool it is using. Having said that, of course, the client understands that best-practice tools are more likely to yield the best results. The more efficient the tool is, the easier it is to use, and so forth, are important factors from the applicant's perspective and from the manager doing the hiring.

"If it was up to BP," Whalley says, "we wouldn't update recruiting tools every three years or so. We're naturally much more interested in drilling wells than in putting cash toward updating our HR kit if it isn't broken. . . . That was why it was important for us to contract with a company for which an essential piece of the business model was to stay at the forefront of HR processes."

A letter of intent was signed in May 1999, culminating in an agreement at year end that covered the following:

- Scope of work: all major transactional processes conducted by HR

    General HR administration, including compensation administration, training administration, compliance (statutory reporting), recruitment and employment contracts administration, internal placement and development support, and job posting

    Payroll administration and processing

    General benefits administration

Retiree administration

Domestic relocation

Expatriate relocation and assignment administration

Provider-vendor management

HRIS–data management, including PeopleSoft, call
center and processing service centers, and interfaces

- Initial employing countries in scope: United States and
United Kingdom, with provision to carry out due diligence on
more countries to progress to a globalized service if appropriate

- Guaranteed savings on direct operating cost of 20 percent
from the sixteenth month of contract, with further gain-share
provision after recovery of defined investment and other
charges by Exult

- Defined intervention and exit provisions in the event of per-
sistent performance failures following activity transfer

- No obligation for transfer of staff to Exult other than specific
BP staff retention arrangements until satisfactory knowledge
transfer achieved

Preparation Work

Over the summer of 1999, after the letter of intent between Exult and
BP was signed but before the transaction was finalized, an Exult team
lead by newly appointed COO Steve Unterberger developed some
mock examples of what the company could potentially provide.

Unterberger and Madden had several meetings with BP executives in London, including with Lord Browne, BP's CEO, who was
particularly intrigued by the idea of a Web-enabled HR department.
(Browne's keen interest in the Web-enablement part of the deal would
later put significant pressure on the transition team to produce results very early in the transition.) Because HR services touch every
employee in an organization, the CEO recognized a Web-enabled
HR service as an effective way of reaching across the organization to
accelerate widespread use of the Web for everyday business activities.

The timing was ideal to take advantage of the common desktop and laptop operating environment recently established throughout the organization.

Dave Latin was soon to be named the e-HR lead at BP. As he recalls, those initial examples went under the rubric of "MyBPA.com." The actual Web presence, the "myHR" brand, was created later by the e-HR team. Latin says the e-HR team "spent the next six months chasing hard to make the vision become a reality, and the first release, which happened just a few months later, was all about trying to do something that looked like what had been shown to the top managers."

BP also went through an extensive buy-in process (referred to as "enrollment") with its business unit leaders in the United States and United Kingdom (approximately 120 people were individually targeted) as part of finalizing the contract. BP wanted its managers to know what the future looked like for HR and how it could have a positive impact on their business. The HR leadership of BP felt that this process would prove to be very important to Exult's ultimate success, especially given the decentralized nature of the company.

Pricing was also negotiated and agreed on—no easy feat, given that neither party had ever priced a package of services like this before (this was an industry first), and BP didn't have a finely honed method for measuring how much it was spending on individual HR services per employee or even per unit. "We had a crude method to determine what we had been spending," Packham says, "But figuring out how much Exult should charge us for each process was difficult, cumbersome. One dark, damp evening in London, toward the end of contract negotiations, we devised a hypothetical pricing distillation device—a 'crystal barrel' into which all HR people cost and activity was loaded. There were only three outlet 'spiggots' or taps—one into a bucket associated with activity going to Exult, a second of activity remaining with BP, and a third into a small bucket of exceptions, which referred to things that were going to stop or were out of scope."

The device worked, but in practice, during the transition phase after contract signing, the process required a few reruns to get the "distillates" to an acceptable level of purity in each bucket for all parties to say, "Let's go with the result." This was a necessary exercise given the radically different service delivery model on which all BP's previous cost allocation mechanisms had operated. In the contract, a minimum initial annual service cost was committed to Exult and in practice, it was exceeded when the "distillation" process had run its course.

Meanwhile, Exult began to staff up. With General Atlantic Partners' approval, Madden hired people who had previously run shared service centers for HP, Kraft, and Sears. He acquired Gunn Partners, a firm that had been doing shared service center design for the previous eight years. He hired HR professionals, HR consultants, and IT people with Web expertise. None of those newly hired were a perfect fit for the business—after all, Exult was creating a new kind of company—but they were among the most knowledgeable people in the world in their particular areas. As Madden says,

> We had to build from scratch the operating model to run the processes. No one knew how to do it. But we were excited and exhilarated, and we relied on our collective, diverse experiences.
>
> Some people feel that to outsource certain aspects of the HR function is to downgrade HR. We felt strongly, going into the deal with BP, that our function was to *upgrade* HR. The idea behind the BPO business is to allow people in the HR area to excel where they want to excel, on value-added components of the business. There's been this tradition of asking people to come into an HR department and excel at operational processes and then gradually move into discretionary areas of counseling, coaching, and organizational change. And there's been this expectation that if you don't move up that path, you're not progressing as you should. The key to a BPO model is to allow the individual to take on the right role with the right training, tools, and focus.

The seven-year contract, which included an option for BP to purchase a 9 percent interest in Exult at two dollars per share, was signed on December 14, 1999. On that day, Exult had fewer than thirty employees; with the BP/Amoco merger underway, it was committing to handling HR processes for some fifty thousand BP employees in the United States and the United Kingdom. (Exult was to be handling about 65 percent of the employees of the new BP; the total number of company employees was about seventy-five thousand in fifty countries.) None of the BP-Amoco HR processes had been standardized or integrated. BP would also shortly acquire Arco, Vastar, and Burmah Castrol, but additions were not an immediate concern for Exult; Burmah Castrol wasn't even a consideration. (As of early 2004, 60,000 employees in the United States and United Kingdom are in the Exult service scope out of 115,000 employees worldwide.) At the time of the contract, all parties thought that the scope of the work would quickly become global.

Implementation

When BP signed on with Exult in December 1999, Exult was a fledgling organization. Madden and his colleagues knew theoretically how to do the work of HR BPO, but there was no body of experience to draw on. There was no list of common mistakes and challenges and no list of best practices to reference. They were managing a start-up that was operating in two uncharted territories: HR BPO and e-HR. Not only didn't they know how to do some things, they didn't know what they didn't know.

BP was a known risk taker, but it too was venturing into uncharted territory. The company's managers were aligned with Exult in terms of commitment and enthusiasm, but they didn't understand the scope of the work at hand. They didn't know what Exult needed in order to do its work correctly and didn't understand, as they do now, the ramifications of trying to standardize and connect all of the various HR processes within BP while at the same time transforming HR units from top to bottom. As Don Packham says,

"We didn't know it at the time, but we handed them a bag filled with snakes."

At the time of the Exult contract, multiple processes were being used to execute each HR process. A classic example showed up in the United Kingdom, where more than one hundred unique employment contracts were in use. Subsequently, they were reduced to ten generic contracts with additional discretionary clauses.

As Kevin Campbell (now COO of Exult) puts it, to say that the learning curve was steep is an understatement. He joined Exult just after the BP contract was signed and now says, "I try not to think about my first few days with the company."

Campbell was better prepared than most others entering the HR BPO field. Before joining Exult, he was head of Ernst & Young's $400 million BPO practice. Before that, he spent almost eighteen years with Accenture, the last nine of them as a partner. In his most recent position there he was responsible for business process management for the resources market unit. Prior to that he had extensive experience with large, complex projects and implementing outsourcing initiatives while serving as the Northeast region's partner for the high-tech and electronic market segments.

Although Campbell had as close to an ideal pedigree for the field of HR BPO as one could have, today he says, "There were no experts to turn to; there were no precedents to consider. No one had done this exact type of thing before, and it felt like walking out onto new ice. It was exhilarating, but that's probably not the term I would have chosen to describe the experience at the time."

Chris Moorhouse, BP group vice president of HR, points out just how tough times got: "There have been times when I've wanted to throw the people from Exult out the window. And I'm sure there have been times when they've felt the same about me. But the high points come when we see the performance statistics. We're making real progress." Similar thoughts come from Jim Madden: "There have been episodes of hand-to-hand combat, with casualties on both sides. But at the end of the day, they are a great partner because they committed, like we did, to the long-term."

The idea was simple and powerful. It was to have the HR function concentrate on the areas where it could add significant value. The approach was to distill HR, to segregate activities within the HR domain so that the people who wanted to pursue matters of strategic contribution could do so unfettered, leaving Exult to handle all of the nondiscretionary matters—the sorts of tangible things that HR generally has to deliver on schedule throughout the year.

In April 2000, Exult began to take over BP's administrative HR processes in the United Kingdom and United States, with the rest of BP's global operations falling into scope soon after. The initial timetable called for Exult to handle transition activity as soon as practicable by one of two routes: first, to take on existing operations where they were and then migrate to Exult's own operations center when ready and, second, to move activity directly to an Exult center when and where practicable to operate a leveraged model immediately. Use of either route was by agreement of the parties according to the circumstances and happened only when a set of predetermined readiness tests had been satisfied. Meanwhile, the e-HR team would begin work on the types of Web processes that BP's top executives had seen and were expecting.

There was an urgency for Exult to achieve the transfer of activity and move it to a leveraged state: the company had just fourteen months from the start of the contract to deliver the direct labor-related services at BP's existing cost less 20 percent. At that stage, BP also had to have delivered a certain minimum level of activity or otherwise pay Exult at the agreed-to minimum service level.

In fourteen months, Exult had to create capability in facilities, systems, and workforce; achieve knowledge transfer; and develop operating process and procedures. This was where the harsh reality of making promises and living up to them for both parties came into play. For Exult, the challenge was to create the capability and get moving on the transition of work. For BP, it was to extract activities from across fragmented processes and work units without critical loss of function or knowledge.

There were problems almost immediately. Very little went as originally planned. As one former Amoco executive puts it, "Exult put forth this huge effort to bite off a huge task, and then they had serious indigestion." Executives from BP and Exult agree, however, that there is little either side could have done to avoid the "initiation rites" of Exult's being the first HR BPO provider of its kind and BP being the first client. Being the first mover has its advantages, but that position also comes with requisite mistakes and a steep learning curve.

As Peter Whalley notes, "You're trying to change a model that essentially has existed for more than fifty years, despite the state it might be in. It has to be done with persistence. You have to grind away and grind away at things." At the time of the contract signing, all parties knew at some level that that was the case, but at the same time, they didn't know it. The promise of what could be bred an enthusiasm that was as contagious as it was potentially misleading.

Web Pressure

The process of moving BP's HR services onto the Web offers perhaps the highest-profile example of how initial expectations have changed as Exult's work with BP has progressed. Initially, managers from both companies were romanced by the notion of an interactive, companywide portal serving up anything HR had to offer to the entire organization. The reality of what could be delivered, and when, was very different.

Clark Cridland, who was accountable for the transition team for BP in the United Kingdom, sums it up this way:

> You have to remember that in 2000, we were overcome by the dot-com buzz. I had just come from a job as HR manager for IT at the time, and I know that it was frantic. There was a sense that there was a "new economy" and an "old economy" and that anything based in the old economy was at a very real risk of collapsing. If a process or a system or a business unit or a company wasn't plugged

into the new economy, it was going to be out. There was this fever, and we all had it. Everything had to be about the Internet. And nothing was going to do except turning ourselves into a dot-com. Web-izing things. Dot-com-ing things. And because the thinking had been that Exult would come in and automate the HR function, well, *automate* really became a synonym for "put it on the Web." And the people at Exult had the fever too.

The result, in Cridland's words, was that the entire project in a sense "got kidnapped." Put another way, Exult's work was seen throughout the company less as a cost-cutting, administration-relieving move and more, as one former manager recalled, as the first step toward making BP over into a new economy, Internet-savvy enterprise. Lord Browne had indicated his interest in the Web-based tools he had seen Exult demonstrate. The rest of the BP corporate board seemed to be similarly enthusiastic.

When the transition team talked with BP's line managers, Cridland remembers, they said things like, "We're going to put HR on the Web. We're going to put HR processes on the Web so that all you have to do is point and click, and this is going to be so great that you're going to live in fear that we won't let you have it."

Looking back, he says, "We were telling the story before we had the opportunity to test whether the scenario was feasible. It wasn't. And that talk came back to bite us, big time. HR's relationship with line managers has seen challenge and difficulty since that time, which I can trace back to the way this was introduced.

Dave Latin was drafted in January 2000 to spearhead what was called the "e-HR" effort from the BP side. Latin, along with Ian Williamson, one of the original team members on the BP side, Exult's Peter Work, who had helped craft the original "demo," and Rebecca Work, then Exult's CIO, concentrated on the e-HR effort. As he recalls, the group at that time didn't know what its first release was going to look like. They had a set of possible products and a deadline of April 14, 2000, but not a specific course.

"Some really good work had been going on before I arrived," Latin says. "But it was a small group of people, and there was a huge mountain to climb. So what we tried to do was to give the semblance of progress without making life impossible for ourselves. We tried to think functionally about what we could deliver over the Web on that time scale. We tried to set on something that would have a 'wow' factor to it but also wouldn't be a complete waste of time and money because we'd have to throw it away a week later."

Latin and his colleagues did manage to deliver a number of things on April 14, 2000, that did indeed have a "wow" factor. Among them was a product called the "International Center" that essentially was a calculator for expatriate employees. An employee living in Aberdeen could go on the Web wondering what it would be like if he or she relocated to Beijing, or what kind of package he or she might get by moving to Houston, and the "center" would access the relevant company policy or expatriate policy for the location in question. The employee could plug in a salary, and the program would calculate his or her pay in the new location, plus housing allowances, travel allowances, and the like. It offered a degree of transparency to BP's expatriate employees that had never been available before, and it streamlined to minutes a process that previously would have taken several weeks of laborious correspondence.

Latin's group also delivered a tool for the high-level sponsors of the project, BP's chair and board, that allowed them to see career details and key data on their senior managers: the top management circle and the company's two hundred or so business unit leaders. The program could pull up vital statistics on this group, including their most recent 360-degree review results, their personal development aspirations, and their career histories.

The big splash in the middle of the summer was the launch in the United States and United Kingdom of a tool called "My Future," which employees could use to learn about and scout for other positions within the organization. Under "My Future," there was My Profile (what the person was currently doing), My Job Market (information about jobs available throughout the company), and My Agent (a tool that would alert employees when jobs were posted that might interest them). "That one came at a good time because of the mergers," Latin recalls. "Suddenly we'd become a big company, and we needed a way to stitch it all together."

But these launches didn't come without pain, and the process served to highlight the massive size of the undertaking. For example, as Latin recalls, "With the tool for the top managers, I went to Irvine, California [Exult's corporate headquarters], when we were testing everything, and we found that all the management comments had gotten mixed up. So you'd have a hypothetical Mr. Wu from China and his 360-degree review feedback was showing up on someone else's report. We had to go line by line to make sure the information was correct. We had just the most appalling time."

More difficult was Latin's experience with a longer-term initiative, "My Data," which was scheduled for release in 2001. The idea was to create a database of people's skills and vital information that would be kept current by the employees themselves. Latin, along with his counterparts at Exult, was concerned that the HR database for the company as a whole wasn't standardized and contained many overlapping segments with conflicting information. He put together a team of people within his group to study what he called "global solutions to people data," an initiative that has not yet come to fruition. "It was like banging my head against a wall for a year," he recalls. Not only was it hard to get a handle on the solution, but it was difficult to get internal funding to sort out the issues once they were identified.

"And to think this was the 'sexy' bit of the project!" Latin notes. "All of the payroll stuff was creating lots of pain and noise in the background, and I was lucky enough not to be involved in that. But at the same time, I sometimes felt as though I was on the tip of the iceberg, because I was the visible face of the whole Exult deal with BP. So if pay slips weren't appearing, it was perceived as being our fault because they called the whole thing the 'e-HR project,' and it seemed as though we were responsible for everything even though we weren't."

As Whalley says, "The contract wasn't drawn around the e-HR effort; it was actually silent on that. The contract was drawn about the transfer of transactional activities, and e-HR was one of the delivery tools. But at times it didn't seem that way. The Web ignited the imagination, but the imagination flies faster than the feet. Today, four years into the contract, we're just beginning to see the e-HR effort really come together. And it will probably take another three years before they get to a smart state. You have to keep in mind that we're trying to transform things that have grown over decades; we're not like a company that is starting from scratch today, integrating IT and the Web as a matter of course."

The Transfer to Exult

"The Iceberg," as Latin referred to it, encompassed the transfer of all of HR's regular, scheduled administrative work for the United States and the United Kingdom from BP to Exult. This included payroll processing and benefits enrollment and administration—the heavy duty must-haves of HR.

Prior to the Exult contract, all of these services had been processed through individual HR departments at each BP site. For example, in the United Kingdom, BP had roughly ten major sites with several hundred or more people working at each of them and many smaller sites. At each major site, HR had some twenty processes in its purview, and it might be handling them in a different way than they were handled at every other site. Now, all of these disparate processes were supposed to be standardized and "go live" with Exult no more than fifteen months after the contract was signed.

To achieve this, Exult had to take several big steps. It had to establish service centers. For the United Kingdom, it had to find a suitable location with appropriate infrastructure and staff it. Glasgow was selected as the best place. In the first six months following contract signing, a facility was selected, leased, and prepared for operation. Few BP employees were willing to transfer to Glasgow, so Exult had to build its own employee base from scratch. In the U.S. Exult had already purchased the Tenneco call center in Woodland, Texas, in order to service the United States. The facility had been a shared service center for Tenneco (when that company was still a conglomerate). As part of that deal, Exult gained two relatively small HR service contracts. Ramping up for BP service delivery cost Exult approximately $40 million.

By the third quarter of 2000, Exult was ready in a broad-stroke kind of way. The problem was that there was an enormous amount of change occurring and just three more quarters to go before the service transition from BP to Exult was contracted for completion.

The plan was that the joint Exult-BP transition team would assess the many ways BP had of doing each HR process and decide on the way the process would be done going forward when Exult took over. Rather than doing the same task in twenty different ways, Exult would have one way to do each process. This was fundamental to the strategy underpinning the Exult-BP deal because it was where Exult would realize the necessary economies of scale. Nevertheless, it did not happen. As Clark Cridland puts it, "We didn't do it. We were busy and distracted, and Exult was struggling with staffing. And all the collapsing of different styles of doing a process didn't happen. We never stopped to think about the implications of letting those things slip because we were in 'compliance mode' rather than 'strategic contribution mode.' We had a schedule to stick to, and we met our transfer deadlines. And so we made a fundamental strategic decision without ever really talking about it. And that was that Exult would take over things just as they were."

For example, BP's chemical plant in Grangemouth, Scotland, had a process of paying allowances for clothing and safety equipment annually. Exult inherited that process and was expected to manage those annual payments. But other BP sites had a process by which they paid the same types of allowances monthly. Exult inherited that process as well. These payment schedules weren't important in BP's big-picture scheme of things, so there was no pressing reason to rationalize the processes into one method. Now there was a pressing reason, but BP and Exult didn't have time to do that kind of work, and so on the transition date, Exult found itself managing multiple systems, with a new staff, from a central location.

"We built a tremendous amount of complexity into Exult's processes," Cridland recalls. "For BP, prior to Exult, it was okay because we were managing the processes at sites with people who knew the processes and the employees. It was localized. But when we put all of that complexity into Exult's center in Glasgow and tried to do it with people who didn't have any specialized knowledge of any site work, well, you can imagine. And when you multiply that scenario out by the number of processes they had to handle . . ."

Exult and BP held a series of knowledge-sharing events in the United States and the United Kingdom, at which managers from both companies were supposed to examine the existing processes and help figure out how the new process should work. But as Clark Cridland puts it, "It was very difficult to persuade people that Exult was something they needed to spend time on. They were an extremely grumpy group of people because they had been told, essentially, that BP's strategy in HR was to outsource the kind of work that they did, and that sooner or later, their jobs were going to go away. They felt that they were being devalued."

Furthermore, the Amoco merger was underway and was taking center stage in terms of BP's managers' time. BP and Amoco both had headquarters in the United States, but after the merger, only one was needed. Senior-level U.S. HR managers at Amoco and BP were facing the tough decisions of which managers and other employees were going to be staying on and which were going to be let go.

The remaining managers were starting to make policy decisions. They were also starting to prioritize and make capital investments to accommodate the newly merged entities. All of those decisions were more important than the HR processes that were turned over to Exult, in many of the senior HR managers' minds. The same issues would be revisited in 2002 with Arco, which also had a U.S. headquarters before the merger.

"Supporting HR in a time of mergers puts a heavy strain on HR systems," according to Packham. "Transactions are needed to reorder organization units, several thousands of severances to process, and common grading and coding conventions to create as a start. Meanwhile, the normal daily events of pay and employee changes go on. It was like a bowl of spaghetti."

While the mergers were occurring, Exult and BP were working to meet an expected launch date. As Don Packham says, "There were many theaters to look at in terms of work to be done. And we had had a rosy picture of how slick and wonderful it would be. Then we found ourselves in the middle of the mess and complexity and reality of making it work. There were too many priorities. It's no wonder we had days when we were really cranky."

There was also some staff turnover and movement at the upper management level in BP's HR department during the time the Exult deal was in the 2000–2001 transition phase. Howard Nelson, formerly vice president of HR for Corporate and Functions at BP, left to join Exult. Nelson was replaced by Clark Cridland. Hilary Ware left BP as well, with Wayne Malik stepping in to replace her as U.S. implementation leader in conjunction with his previous role as overall project leader.

All parties attest that the staff movement was handled as smoothly and professionally as possible, yet these changes had an unsettling effect on the project as a whole. It lent an air of instability to a situation that was already confusing to some and threatening to many. For example, as Cridland notes, the "grumpiness" was exacerbated in the group of managers he inherited when he moved to the corporate and functions HR office (the HR department responsible for everything HR that wasn't in one of the company's business units), because the project had literally been a source of problems every day. Cridland reflects, "It was a difficult situation. There was a lot of tension in the team, and it only intensified as April [2001] drew near."

Jim Madden sums it up this way:

> Our clients are not homogeneous organizations. There are three distinct groups of people within each client company. You have the senior executive suite—our executive sponsors. They had the courage and the chutzpah to do this. Then you have the consumers of the system—the employees of the company at large—and we should be invisible to them. We should be behind the scenes, and what they should notice is that things are getting done faster, things are easier to do with regard to their contacts with HR. Then you have the third group, the HR managers. These are the people whose head counts are being rearranged. They are the toughest group to move along in this, and one of the biggest lessons we learned is that we needed to do a better job of change management to let that group know what its role can be in a postoutsourcing world.

The people who had much of the HR operations knowledge at BP were scheduled to become redundant at BP as a result of the Exult contract. Exult needed these same individuals to help it understand how the old system had worked (and also its flaws) so that the new system could accommodate and compensate as needed. But the pace in HR and throughout the company was frantic, and many midlevel HR managers at BP were suspicious of Exult at best. At times it seemed to them that there weren't enough Exult staff on hand to receive the knowledge. The pace inside Exult was similarly frantic: Exult had a promised deadline to meet, and it was in the process of going public.

As Whalley explains, the knowledge that had to be transferred from BP to Exult was spread over some six hundred to seven hundred people who together made up the equivalent of four hundred full-time employees. Exult did not employ four hundred people, and it had hired only a handful of BP employees at the time. "The challenge for Exult," Whalley sums up, "was how to extract enough knowledge from the BP group to ensure that the business wouldn't crash in the hands of complete strangers. Exult and BP had to motivate people to hand over knowledge when those people knew that doing so would mean losing their jobs down the line."

Then there were the data. As Exult's Kevin Campbell says, BP's own organizational complexity kept tripping up the works. "We were not only taking BP to Exult, but also we were taking the work of HR from individual business units in the United States and United Kingdom to our centralized centers. BP to this day is unique because it believes that the power in its model lies in its autonomous business units. BP wants the benefits of scale—and strives to get the benefits of scale—but it also wants its business units to be able to do things in their own way. It's a tough balancing act, and certainly one that would be difficult to replicate."

The payroll transition from BP was the toughest Exult has been through. In the United Kingdom, small glitches occurred all over the place. In the throes of stitching together a single system from some three individual systems in the United Kingdom, Exult now had to go back and learn how certain mistakes or individual idiosyncrasies had been "hand-tweaked" in the past to make the process run smoothly.

Cridland recalls a particular low point, early on in Exult's work, when employees in one group were overpaid dramatically for several months. "It was terrible," Cridland says. "It was a site where employees were represented by a union, and figuring out how to manage the process, how the money would be recovered, *who* would manage the process . . . It was a major industrial relations disruption at that site."

Packham counts the switchover days for the two biggest conversion projects in the United States as the two lowest points of his experience working with Exult. On the day when Amoco and Arco payrolls were to be handled by Exult for the first time, the company did lose timeliness and accuracy despite everyone's hard work. (Amoco moved on December 31, 2001, to Exult; Arco moved on December 31, 2002.) There were twenty thousand employees in Amoco at the time, and some seventeen thousand in Arco. And as Packham says, when the paychecks went out, "Literally the phones lit up and the e-mails started piling up."

The problems had to be fixed one by one, a time-consuming and often frustrating exercise. Sometimes it was easy to spot the glitch; the managers were relieved when the problem was something that they could spot across several mistakes and correct with one maneuver. Often, though, the mistakes had to be corrected individually.

Moreover, there were delays that made sense logically but were unexpected. For example, checks issued out of Houston and mailed to employees took longer to deliver than checks that previously had been mailed out of Tulsa.

Packham is quick to point out that even if the company had had more resources and more time to spend on the transition, he's not sure it would have gone any more smoothly. "These are heritage systems of complexities," he says. "The IT system that feeds payroll has to do many things. If you're dismantling an old system and plugging in a new one and you don't get it exactly right in the connections, you're going to see some things that don't work when you flip the switch."

Heritage BP was on PeopleSoft; Amoco was on Tesseract; and Arco, Vastar, and Burmah were on Bespoke Systems. There were hundreds of interfaces for systems between business units, third-party providers, taxing, and compliance authorities. The low points were mentally draining. "We knew we just had to slog our way through it," Packham says. "But it wasn't something you'd sign up for." Cridland adds,

> We had a trust issue eventually. First, many BP managers and employees perceived that the mistakes they were seeing would not have happened if the people who had done the work forever on-site were still there. So people were questioning the fundamental strategy of the project. Second, many of the mistakes appeared to be stupid mistakes to people who had worked at BP for a long time and understood the company and its processes. Exult would always fix the mistake quickly and politely, and often in a way so that it never recurred, but the seed had been planted that there was something fundamentally wrong with HR's strategy and the way it was being managed.

What a wonderful, glowing story we'd told. And this period in the summer of 2001 was when everyone realized that the story wasn't true. In the employees' and line managers' views, we were replacing slightly clunky processes with particularly clunky processes. And because it was all supposed to be more self-service oriented, our line managers felt that HR had been outsourced all right— outsourced to *them*.

Before, if you wanted to move an employee from A to B, you'd make a call to BP HR and they'd do it. Now they had to call Exult and Exult would ask them to fill out forms—job codes, employee numbers, and so on. They may have been responsible for all those codes and numbers previously, but they were not used to using them. It appeared to them that they were the ones doing the bulk of the work. It caused a real crisis of confidence.

That crisis reached a point that whenever anything went wrong relating to an HR issue, line managers and the community at large in BP considered Exult to be the culprit. "It's a fact that 50 percent of the problems that were attributed to Exult's performance came from BP," Cridland says. For example, when someone reached a significant service date anniversary at BP, that person received recognition, and Exult handled the recognition process. But if the entry was wrong in the database, then Exult would get it wrong and be blamed for the error even though it wasn't its mistake. "That's what we were contending with," Cridland says. "People in HR at BP knew these things and knew how to compensate for data errors. But Exult, which had to rely on the process, got blamed. And it is still happening to this day. About half of the performance difficulties have a basis in a preexisting problem with data in BP."

Regaining Trust

The BP-Exult relationship reached its lowest point in fall 2001, when the companies experienced near-crises on a number of HR service delivery fronts, most notably with the BP expatriate team in

London. This group had the least robust data and processes and was paying for that lack as Exult struggled to get their arms around information that had largely resided in people's heads until Exult started work. "There was a real potential that the expatriate process was going to lock up. We felt that we were on the edge of an abyss," Cridland says. Then two things happened. First, the head of expatriate services for Exult resigned. Second, Exult and BP put extra people on the project to see the unit through the crisis. "We seriously considered bringing this work back into BP at that point," Cridland says. "But we formed a task force, and Exult put more people on the job, and we pulled back from the edge of the abyss."

At Cridland explains it, that was the period during which people on both sides—throughout Exult and HR at BP—realized that the problems they were experiencing with data accuracy and service delivery weren't going to go away quickly, and the dream of the self-service, flawless HR function, with senior managers free to counsel the corporation at a strategic level, was not going to be realized any time soon.

We cannot report a silver-bullet panacea that solved the data issues. By all accounts, it has been a slow, steady process of building trust, honing the processes, and trying to identify root cause problems so that when mistakes are fixed, they don't reoccur.

Cridland and several others say that Chris Moorhouse, Nick Starritt's successor as group vice president for HR (effective August 2001), helped everyone regain (or, in fact, gain for the first time) perspective on the project and the good things it could accomplish. According to Cridland, "It was Chris who suggested to us that what we needed as a team was to stop and look at where we were with the strategy and the Exult relationship. We needed to recognize what we had set out to do and what had happened, and we needed to be clear about what had not happened and to let it go. He helped us see that we needed to set a course for what we were going to do, set reasonable goals, and manage going forward."

Moorhouse, in other words, helped the BP and Exult teams reset their expectations in the context of the larger, more complex organization that BP had become and also in the context of the notable progress that had already been made. "His perspective was incredibly useful," Cridland reflects:

> It had all become difficult, and it wasn't obvious what the way out might be. People were angry, and they weren't sure where it was going to end. He [Moorhouse] brought the entire HR leadership team from BP together at an off-site meeting without the Exult people, and we talked it through. As a result of that conversation, we were able to bring clarity to ourselves and to Exult. First, we recognized that although the project had been intended as a global strategy, that wasn't realistic. We realized that we needed to focus on the United Kingdom and the United States, and that we had in fact crossed the bridge with Exult in those geographies, but that neither we nor Exult was really equipped or interested in going anywhere else. We also got clear on where accountability would lie. We [the HR leaders] took ownership of the project on behalf of BP in a way that we had not previously done."

In the first six months of 2003, the entire HR department in BP restructured into a front-back organization. It is now aligned as a business function with clear supply- and demand-side activities. The Exult contract is part of the "supply" side; BP managers are employing tools and concepts such as Six Sigma to define roles, set expectations, and measure results. The clarity is increasingly valuable, Whalley says, because it helps keep things in perspective and allows clearer distinction of the roles of HR business managers and HR function operations managers.

Business managers can now focus on the more discretionary demand side of work, and HR function operations managers can focus on delivery of commitments. The new structure also clarifies the business process outsource relationship with Exult as a critical part of the HR function's accountability and capability for delivery of HR promises and commitment to employees and managers across the businesses in the United States and United Kingdom.

Cridland says, and others agree, that "things have gotten slowly better as underlying problems have been fixed. The rate of errors is down. The noise level in BP had gone down. Management is more comfortable that things are heading in the right direction. Everyone is aware that the progress is incremental and is comfortable with that situation."

Results

The major results of the Exult-BP partnership include the following:

• Operating cost savings are gaining year-on-year. As of 2003, they are worth in excess of $15 million a year compared to the baseline operating cost.

• BP has achieved a more strategic focus in its HR function. HR senior management is harnessing knowledge about employees' expertise and goals and aligning deployment of people with the company's strategy. Operations metrics now abound to help identify improvement opportunities and prioritize actions.

• BP has avoided capital expenditures (which would have been more than $30 million) on service centers, process management controls systems, transition setup, and e-HR portal development.

• The efficiency of processes, response times, and reliability of action for the HR transactions in Exult's scope have improved.

• Several HR processes are electronically enabled: the e-HR portal, now called myHR, is delivering information and Web-enabled HR services to BP employees. BP has made significant progress toward getting most of its English-speaking employees to use the Web (see Figure 6.1).

At the end of 2003, twenty-five thousand people were accessing myHR each month, an increase of about 10 percent compared to a year earlier. The most widely accessed section within myHR is myJobMarket, where internal jobs are posted and applied for. Through October 2003, over fifty-five hundred jobs had been posted, and over seventeen thousand people had applied on-line for them. Over 350,000 myAgent e-mails had been sent.

Figure 6.1 Employee Use of myHR.net at BP

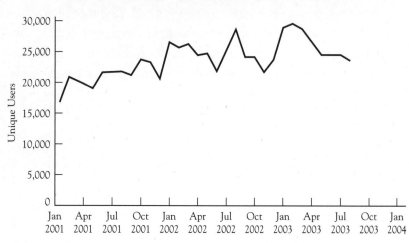

Employee self-service is widely used in the United States and United Kingdom, where people change their personal details, direct deposit information, or emergency contact information on-line. Currently 70 to 80 percent of these changes are made on-line versus calling Exult. Manager self-service, implemented in the United Kingdom in November 2002, provides on-line capability for making changes to employee status, spot bonuses, transfers, leaves of absence, and promotions. Today over 95 percent of these transactions are made on-line. Service delivery is set up differently in the United States, where manager self-service is not yet used.

- In September 2003, a survey of one thousand randomly selected users of myHR was made. Ninety-two percent were neutral to very satisfied, and 8 percent were dissatisfied with myHR. The majority of the written comments were very positive, yet some expressed concern about not speaking with a "real person" or on-line privacy and security.

- The business integrations of Amoco, Arco, Vastar, and Burmah Castrol were accelerated as a result of their using common HR processes and measures.

• Although Exult has delivered cost savings to BP, they did not come as quickly and are below the middle of the range originally hoped for. Expectations have been revised and realigned with what has proven to be a more realistic understanding of how the work gets done. However, accelerated integration of additional business from the mergers and acquisitions has offset the immediate economic shortfall on the original business case, and achieving the longer-term operating savings promised remains possible.

• Customer satisfaction levels regarding HR services (as reported by BP employees, managers, and the HR community) have improved. The satisfied customer level for HR services has gained at least 15 percentage points since just prior to contract in both the United States and United Kingdom and is now continuously measured. Table 6.1, which presents the data for the United States, shows an improving level of employee satisfaction.

The BP HR staff-to-employees ratio has increased from a ratio of approximately 1:60 at the start of 2000 to a level of around 1:80 in 2003. Not all of this is attributable to the U.S. and U.K. outsourcing initiative, but it is a significant contributor. The total employee base has increased some 30 percent in that period because of the mergers and acquisitions.

Table 6.1 BP Employee Satisfaction with HR Service Levels, United States, 2002–2003

BP U.S. Customer Satisfaction	Second Quarter, 2002	Third Quarter, 2002	Fourth Quarter, 2002	First Quarter, 2003
Very satisfied	28%	43%	46%	49%
Satisfied	28	26	29	25
Neither satisfied nor dissatisfied	14	9	9	6
Dissatisfied	14	11	8	9
Very dissatisfied	14	12	8	12

- The potential global scope of the arrangement proved too ambitious, and expectations were revised in early 2001. As Don Packham says, "Originally, we conceived of it [the Exult model] going everywhere. But in a country with, say, only two hundred BP employees, you just can't make the cost-benefit equation work." Former Amoco, Arco, and Burmah Castrol employees are now all on the same systems as BP employees in the United States and United Kingdom. Exult currently handles what would originally have been $45 million of BP annual direct cost in HR staff and IT costs. Exult also provides supply chain management on a further $80 million of annual third-party HR-related contract services to BP.

- BP is still dealing with some excess capacity. After Exult's service centers opened, BP in theory had four hundred excess full-time equivalents. But initially, the company was uneasy about reducing the staff, feeling that they needed to have the backup resources on hand if Exult's efforts derailed. "At the time, the company felt the need to hedge its bets," says Whalley. "It was at business discretion as to how much additional resource was retained and for how long. No one was left idle post-transition as business demand expanded to fill the capacity and transition issues were addressed; however, demand management is a key part of the newly emerging function."

- BP has much more standardized HR processes and, as a result, better measures. As John Hannacher, U.K. operations manager notes, "The relationship with Exult has certainly enabled us to make progress on simplification and standardization of processes, which we would probably not have done otherwise. I am thinking of the development of the single U.K. employment contract as an example where a good working relationship has certainly played its part. We also now have more data and measures on the delivery of HR transactions than we ever had before."

Tom Macartney, the U.S. operations manager for BP, adds, "Exult has worked closely with BP in a very partner-oriented manner to ensure the development of a strong performance management process incorporating detailed metrics, monthly performance discussions with the organization, as well as formal quarterly performance reviews. Good, open working relationships have been a vital factor. As a result of the outsourcing of transactional HR activity, BP today has a huge amount of objective data around HR transactional delivery that was not previously available."

Lessons Learned

Both BP and Exult managers admit that their initial expectations—about the scope of work Exult should take on, how difficult that work would be to transfer, and how much progress to expect during a given period of time—were overly optimistic and in some cases way off the mark.

Yet most managers we interviewed who were involved with the project acknowledge that given the fact that the two companies were breaking ground in a new industry and given that BP is a very large, decentralized organization, the process went almost as smoothly as could have been expected. It is fair to say that BP was an extremely challenging first customer for Exult. On a scale of 1 to 10, it was an 8 or 9 level of difficulty. The fact that HR BPO is successful in BP says a great deal about the value of the approach. It also provided a great deal of learning for Exult and gave it a sense that it could succeed with the most challenging customers.

It took Exult and BP eighteen months to get through what both would call the initial transition phase, in which work was moved from BP to Exult. Today, that amount of time would be completely unacceptable; HR BPO providers—and client companies—demand a much shorter start-up period. But as Peter Whalley, of BP says, for a start-up in a fledgling industry, working with a company as large and as complex as BP, the transition period "really was not a surprise."

As Whalley and other managers from BP and from Exult explain, the complexity of the project was not something that either group could have understood when they started work, no matter how much time they had spent preparing. For example, Exult could not have anticipated the amount of data being "hand-tweaked" on a daily basis in all of BP's many separate HR units to ensure that payroll and benefits were administered correctly.

There was a great deal of tacit knowledge within BP at the beginning of its work with Exult; that knowledge needed to be made explicit in order for Exult to be able to perform the basic administrative tasks without a hitch, Exult and BP to be comfortable reducing costs by reducing the BP HR workforce (thereby potentially letting tacit knowledge escape), Exult and BP to move any processes onto the Web successfully, and Exult to be able to track costs and measure progress.

Reflecting, Dave Latin takes pride in what he was able to accomplish, and he feels that the lessons that his group learned are important and transferable. "You need to understand the state of your system," he says. "If the underlying systems are a mess, there's only so much you can do with a Web overlay. Where practical, you want your users to update the data for you. But at the same time, you can't keep going back every week to the user for something else. You have to think very carefully about your strategy. You've got your early adapters, and you've got the people who will never adapt. And what you have to do is identify the early adapters and use them to help pull more and more people onto the bandwagon."

When Clark Cridland reflects on lessons learned, his emphasis is on change management and communication: "Getting the HR community engaged was probably one of the things that we fell down on in a way that made it difficult for us later on."

Cridland and Packham, when asked about HRO relationships in general, point to the information going to Exult, or to any other outsourcer for that matter. "If the company isn't providing accurate data, the outsourcer is going to have a problem," Packham says. The whole supply chain, in other words, is only as good as its weakest link.

Moorhouse similarly points out the need to make tacit knowledge explicit. "If you take the expatriation area as an example," he explains, "a lot used to get done because individual people knew how to do it. But when it came time to look for documentation, it wasn't always complete. The process really should be transparent before it is transferred."

Conclusions

There is unmistakable, measurable progress and positive results. Both companies' representatives say they are pleased overall. As Packham explains, the big mental rewards come when the two groups step back for their quarterly performance reviews. "That's when you see how the daily work becomes the big picture," he says. At these reviews, the Exult managers get together with business leaders and senior HR managers at BP and examine what has been happening, how the numbers are evolving, and what the goals are for the next quarter and beyond. "We find ourselves feeling very good when we realize we're having productive conversations about service delivery and company strategy," Packham says. "You can't do that with any other model; you can't see the results in totality the way we can and you can't affect change on the scale and in the manner we can. When we talk about service delivery, we're able to see something as a whole that in most companies is fragmented. We have a chance to apply innovative thinking and technology improvement across the board; other companies can't do that."

Moorhouse notes, "Payroll timing and accuracy is always difficult. Before Exult, we didn't know what our timing and accuracy levels were because we didn't have the data to track. We didn't track when mistakes were being made; we fixed them and then likely as not fixed them again the next time around. There was no way to identify root cause problems, and if we always managed to help the customer get things right quickly, that's fine, but we weren't preventing errors from happening again, the way we are now."

Says Whalley, with the perspective that time brings,

> Looking back, the transition period really wasn't all that long, considering how far we've come. It was only painful for about twelve months, and the marketplace was reading the noise as well, so it probably seemed even more intense from the outside than it was. But the big prizes are now coming through. We can do things we couldn't have dreamed of doing three years ago. People are struggling to figure out what their new roles are going to be, but when we

contemplate new initiatives, we have cumulative data to figure out what resources are going to be required and what impact a change is having. Looking forward, for example, we're contemplating with Exult the possibility of going 24/7 with HR services, and we have a clear picture of what it would take and how to go about it.

Chris Moorhouse concludes, "We took a bold step and now see that with Exult, we have created a new market. We are just beginning to experience and explore a new and valuable range of possibilities for HR service delivery."

Chapter Seven

Bank of America

Business: Financial services

Contract signing: November 2000

Contract term: Ten years

Contract value: $1.1 billion, plus a $600 million add-on signed in September 2001

Geographical coverage: United States

Employees in company: 150,000

Employees covered: Approximately 145,000 at contract signing

Scope of BPO contract: Payroll, recruiting, HR IT, accounts payable, employee expense reimbursement, benefits administration, expatriate administration, "life event" coordination (leaves of absence and retirement); also technology support and third-party vendor management related to those functions

Less than a year after Exult contracted with BP, and while Exult and BP were still learning how best to work together, Exult gained another significant client. It signed the Bank of America to a ten-year contract.

Bob Gunn was responsible for the initial contact. Gunn had been working since 1994 in the areas of finance and personnel for NationsBank, which subsequently merged with BankAmerica to form Bank of America. He had a professional and personal friendship with Marc Oken, who was the chief accounting officer at Bank of America. In the spring of 2000, Exult was trying to put together a deal with CitiBank, but it fell through in May. Gunn at that point introduced Jim Madden to Marc Oken.

For Exult, the attraction of the deal was clear: BP had put Exult on the map, but a contract with a major financial institution would validate the business model and give Exult the chance to show that it was a viable commercial entity, able to handle more than a single (albeit large and complex) client. As Kevin Campbell reflects, "BP is known as a risk taker, so when BP signed with Exult, some companies and analysts dismissed the deal as just another BP gamble. Once we added Bank of America to our client list, those same folks could no longer say we couldn't handle a large, top-tier employer as a client."

For the bank, Exult was in the right place at the right time, offering a way to help the bank achieve its strategic goals. The bank had gone through several significant mergers and acquisitions (its merger with NationsBank was the largest and most recent) and was still in the process of meshing several cultures and visions into one. Top managers, led by board chairman Ken Lewis, wanted to shift the institution's focus away from growth through mergers toward growth through leveraging its account base. (Lewis took over as chairman when Hugh McCall retired after the merger of BankAmerica and NationsBank.)

Lewis wanted to create a strategically focused organization and saw Web enablement through an employee portal as a significant step toward that goal. The idea was that the more engaged employees were on the Web for their own HR-related activities, as well as for their work with customers, the more integrated the efforts of the bank would be overall, and the more responsive it could be to a growing customer base.

In HR, senior leaders were aligned with that strategic direction. They were aware that they had built a strong HR team as a result of the mergers. The HR leaders were extremely capable when it came to consolidating back office operations, and standardizing and simplifying functions. As one HR manager recalls, "If this group wasn't doing a merger, they got bored." But they were also aware that they needed to focus on the bank's new vision of an integrated organization. They were looking for new ways to add value and agreed that creation of an employee portal was an important step. They saw Exult as a company that could help accelerate the process of making that portal a reality.

Another HR manager explains the situation at the bank in this way:

> Other companies use outsourcing as a way to force their HR generalists to become strategic. Outsourcing is a first step, taken with cost reduction as the primary driver. The strategy trails behind, and top managers just hope that HR managers will see that they need to contribute strategically. With the bank, outsourcing was really the last piece of the puzzle.
>
> The leaders in HR understood the strategic needs of the organization. We knew that, for our part, we needed to continue to develop staffing strategies, compensation strategies, and development strategies that would strengthen the bank's ability to attract and motivate a world-class workforce. And we understood that although the administrative side of HR was accustomed to taking out costs, we needed more than that in terms of administrative capability. It was sort of a chicken-or-egg situation: we knew that in order to sustain the success of the mergers, we had to focus on administration. But if we took the time to focus on administration and really make that our area of expertise, we would fall behind in our efforts to support the company's strategy. Outsourcing HR administration was a piece of our solution, not our first move.

Due Diligence

The initial meeting between Jim Madden and Marc Oken in 2000 went well. The two found it easy to identify common ground in their business philosophies. On the strength of that meeting, Madden and Gunn put together a proposal letter that mapped out several possible scenarios for a relationship between the bank and Exult.

The letter included an estimate of what Exult could do within four months of a signed contract, within eight months, and further down the line. Madden and Gunn also invited the bank's senior HR executives, including Oken and Steele Alphin, the bank's senior HR executive, to Exult's Houston call center, which was under construction.

As Gunn recalls, "The intangibles were very important, in those early meetings, especially in Houston. The ability for the two groups to talk about the future, and then find a common way to articulate how that future might look, was critical. The bank's HR leadership group had a lot of confidence. And I think they got that same sense of confidence from us."

The tenor of the high-level talks was positive; the next step was due diligence. Exult's Madden and Campbell had learned from their experience with BP the importance of continuity from the sales stage of a contract through implementation and beyond, so they quickly passed the reins of the to-be-determined relationship to their newly appointed sales director, Mike Salvino. Salvino, they agreed, would be the Exult person in charge of the Bank of America relationship through implementation.

Looking back, Salvino recalls that he was given the responsibility for the Bank of America relationship, and all the details, his first day on the job. "I had worked for Kevin Campbell for five years at Accenture," he notes. "Kevin joined Exult in May 2000, and I followed him there in June. There was no ramping-up time; I walked in, and they handed me the letter of intent and sent me off to the bank's headquarters in Charlotte [North Carolina]."

In Charlotte, Salvino met Mary Lou Cagle and Kim Hains, HR managers who reported to Steele Alphin. Salvino, along with Cagle and Hains, were charged with taking the letter of intent and figuring out what would go into a contract.

From Exult's perspective, this due diligence process was a way of determining the mechanics of the potential deal. What would Exult be walking into if it took on the bank's HR administrative responsibilities? How would Exult go about taking on those tasks? How well prepared was the bank for such a transition? What would need to be done initially to make the implementation work? What would need to be done down the line? Exult had already learned a lot from its experiences with BP about how it could best do the work it set out to do and about the essential criteria for success. Salvino, with support from Madden, brought that knowledge to the table in his preliminary work with the bank. He knew, for example, to probe the accuracy of the company's data; he had a good idea of how long the conversions would take and in what order to take them on. He also knew that in order to ensure success, Exult would do well to hire the five hundred or so employees in the bank's HR and accounts payable departments.

From the bank's perspective, the period of consideration was largely centered on minimizing risk. Was Exult's business model solid? Would Exult be around in a year? Two years? Five years? How could the bank structure a deal so that it could be supportive of Exult, while at the same time ensuring that it wouldn't be hurt too badly if things didn't work out? Did Exult truly understand the nuances of the bank's administrative systems? Could this small company handle the volume? Would it able to assimilate so many new employees at once?

As Gunn reflects, the due diligence process was as thorough as he had ever seen: "They sent Price Waterhouse down to look at our financials, and it was like seeing a dermatologist; you really have to undress in front of these guys." He noted that Bank of America also did a quick but extensive search for other companies that might be able to provide the same services that Exult was offering during that time. "In about six weeks, they talked with twelve potential competitors," Gunn says. "They knew what was out there, and that helped them set realistic expectations."

The due diligence process was also a good way to determine whether the connection that the senior executives had made could also be established among the group of people who would be taking the deal through implementation. As Salvino says, "You really can't underestimate how important it was for us to find out that we could work together effectively during the due diligence process. These were the same people who would be working together once the contract was signed. If we had clashed—if our work styles weren't compatible—that would have been a red flag."

To that point, Gunn recalls a meeting he had with Marc Oken midway through the process. "We had breakfast," Gunn said, "and I remember that Marc asked me, 'Who are you going to get to run this?' The question surprised me, because it told me he was ready to operationalize even though we were still in selling mode. But he knew it wasn't going to be me, and he knew it wasn't going to be Jim. I told him it would be Mike Salvino, and he was fine with that. I think that was the point at which I really felt the relationship was a 'go.'"

Gunn explains that from his work with NationsBank, he had come to understand that it was characteristic of the bank to spend a lot of high-level time figuring out what they were going to do, but that once that decision was made, they didn't tend to spend a lot of time figuring out how or when to do it. According to Gunn,

> They tend to cut right to the question, "Who's going to do it?" Marc [Oken], Steele [Alphin], and the other top managers there got very good at assessing talent and picking the right people to handle those details. They had high standards of performance, but they were willing to give people a tremendous range in what they could do to meet those standards. The outcomes were expected, but there was a lot of freedom regarding how to get there.
>
> With Mike, I think they sized him up and said, "Right, he's the person." They could see that the chemistry was good; they could see that he had a passion for the job, and they put their faith in him to carry out the plan as they intended.

At one point after the contract was signed but early on in the relationship, Gunn reports that Alphin told Salvino, "When you are out in front of the bank's employees, remember that you're speaking for me." As Gunn recalls, "Mike was really blown away by that. It was a heck of a responsibility, and it really raised the performance bar for Mike. I think it also shifted his perspective a little as well and made him realize that he should get much more knowledgeable about what the bank was all about, so that he could speak to a much fuller context." Ultimately, Gunn says, that one comment benefited Exult as a whole; it reemphasized how important it was and would continue to be for Exult to work alongside its clients rather than simply working for them.

Contract

By November 2000, the details of the contract were finalized. And on November 21, the bank signed a contract with Exult. Bank of America had $689 billion in assets when it signed with Exult, with full-service operations in twenty-one states and the District of Columbia. Before the acquisition of FleetBoston in 2004, it provided financial products and services to a customer base of approximately 30 million households and 2 million businesses, as well as international corporate financial services for business transactions in 190 countries.

The contract calls for Exult to take on the administration of Bank of America's benefits, payroll, accounts payable, travel and expense accounting, all of HR IT, and the contact (call) center. The terms are a ten-year engagement worth a little over $100 million annually. The initial goal was an annual cost savings to the bank in excess of 10 percent in the functions covered. The bank agreed to shoulder some risk, acquiring 5 million shares of Exult common stock and a warrant to purchase an additional 5 million shares. The contract included a plan and schedule for the creation and launch of the bank's Web portal. For each process, the contract also called for a host of ongoing performance measures to track service delivery levels (speed and accuracy), as well as customer satisfaction levels. The deal positioned Bank of America as Exult's preferred financial services partner to provide financial services and products to Exult's other clients through Exult's own personalized HR Web portal.

One way to consider what the contract called for in greater detail, and to begin to examine the implementation process, is to think of the deal as having four platforms:

- The equity transaction.
- The transfer of BPO tasks, which included the transition of the five hundred employees from the bank's HR and accounts payable departments to Exult. Exult was also picking up Bank of America facilities in Charlotte and in Ellinwood, California, plus several satellite locations providing IT support (for a total of approximately seven hundred new employees).
- The engagement of the bank as Exult's financial services partner, which meant that Exult would be able and expected to offer the bank's services (discounted loans, discounted mortgages, credit cards and so forth) to existing and future clients.
- A Web deal, in which Exult agreed to put its technology into a company the bank had started up to handle its portal.

Until the FleetBoston acquisition, the only significant departure from the original plan concerns the Web portal arrangement with Broadvision Software. The company fell prey to the dot-com implosion and the failing economy. The bank and Exult subsequently revised their agreement: the bank purchased the Exult Web enablement capability, and a team of bank and Exult employees implemented the portal for the bank.

As part of the negotiation process, Salvino, Cagle, Hains, and the rest of their team broke down the four platforms into phases and tasks and mapped out a schedule of expected transitions. They identified people on the Exult side and people on the bank side who were responsible for the individual transitions. And they also adopted a mantra for the first year of the relationship: "Business As Usual." That is, they agreed on an overarching goal that called for the work to be invisible to the bank's employees. A base commitment on both sides was the uninterrupted delivery of the services the employees were used to receiving.

Phase One encompassed accounts payable, payroll, IT, the call centers, and benefits administration. The first area they worked on was accounts payable. As Cagle recalls, on the day after the contract was signed, the transition team started to communicate with the bank associates who would be affected, most of them by being moved from Bank of America to Exult. "We stood in front of each and every one of them," Cagle says, "either in small groups or one-on-one, to talk about what was going to happen and when. We tried to be proactive, addressing any and all of the concerns that we could."

There were many concerns. These people had been identified to move from a large, stable, old institution to a virtual start-up. Some were excited; most were apprehensive. What would happen to their existing benefit and retirement packages? Was the new company a viable entity? Was there a way to opt out?

John Moore, the senior vice president of accounts payable and fixed assets accounting for the bank (today he is Exult's general manager of finance and pay processing in the Charlotte center), credits the ongoing communications efforts with helping to ease the transition pain. Moore, who was brought into the process as Exult and the bank were conducting due diligence, was also initially wary of the new company and the developing plan of action, but he quickly became convinced that HR BPO was a good idea, and Exult had the requisite capabilities. He then became instrumental in the transition effort. Moore noted:

> I had been at the bank for twelve years, and my initial reaction to Exult during the due diligence process had been, "Who are these people, and why do they think they can do this?" But most of the department heads felt that way, and as we learned more, our view started to change from, "I don't believe they can do this," to "Wow, they can do this, and it will be exciting to be a part of it because we'll be moving from a back office function to the front office. We'll be generating revenue."
>
> They educated everybody. The transition team started with the department heads like myself, and then we joined in going throughout

our units, helping people understand the rationale for the change, what Exult was, what its values were, how those values were in sync with the bank's values. They—we—talked about why the bank chose Exult, and what the change would mean for every single employee.

For example, Moore says, he was able to put the benefits packages offered by the bank and by Exult side by side so the personnel moving to Exult could see exactly where they overlapped and where they did not. In many cases, he noted, Exult matched the bank's unique benefits, such as tuition reimbursement.

Moore also participated in many question-and-answer sessions, in which department managers who were moving to Exult would facilitate discussions between Exult's senior managers, such as Campbell and Salvino, and the people slated to move from the bank to Exult. A typical session would involve a group of about thirty employees. Moore would break them up into smaller groups. Often he had people write down their concerns, and then Campbell and Salvino would address the comments. According to Moore, "They opened themselves up to very direct questions. That's one of the reasons people were reassured."

The transition team worked to ensure that the move went smoothly in terms of payroll by scheduling the transition so that they got a full paycheck from the bank on their last pay date there and a full paycheck from Exult on their first pay date with Exult. "Fortunately, the bank pays twice a month, and Exult pays every two weeks, so there were a few points in the year where we could line it up perfectly," Moore says. "These were relatively little things, but they went a long way toward making the transition less nerve-wracking for people."

In truth, Moore says, the technical aspects of the transition were easy when compared with the individual concerns of the employees making the move. Exult addressed their concerns one at a time. ("I'm close to retirement; will Exult bridge that for me?" "What if I don't want to make the move? Will I get severance?")

Mike Salvino agrees with Moore's assessment: "On a Friday in January 2001, 170 people went home as Bank of America employees. On Monday, they came back to work—to the same exact location—as Exult's newest employees. But the hard part wasn't the physical transition, even though we renovated the entire space over a single weekend. It was the stuff that occurred below the surface." Salvino is referring to addressing the worries of Exult's newest employees and, just as important, embedding a new mind-set in that group of people. Before, they had been internal employees serving internal customers. They had been a cost center. Suddenly, they were a profit center, serving one client, with the understanding that they would soon be serving more.

"That meant a lot of small changes in the way we operated," Moore says. "For example, Exult has a more structured service delivery model than we were used to working with. Typically, at the bank, people didn't come to me when things were going well; they came to me only when they had issues. But we never had a formal tracking mechanism to see what needed to be fixed and how often; we just did it. At Exult, there was a tracking tool, and we began to conduct trend analyses of our work all the time."

Moore explains that in practice, the work felt more formal than it ever had before. Whenever something went wrong with an HR process at the bank, the affected employee would call someone in HR, who would fix the problem. Sometimes the problem was fixed quickly; sometimes it took more time. Service delivery was inconsistent. And it was always possible that the same problem would resurface several times.

Exult required that when a bank employee, or "client," called with a problem, the question or complaint had to be addressed formally and be routed to the contact center. Sometimes the process took longer than it would have previously. But as Moore notes, "This way, we could ensure that the client wouldn't encounter the same problem again the following week, or month, or year. And others wouldn't either. We learned that if you see a number of glitches in a particular area, you don't just fix them; you look for the root cause."

As Moore recalls, "The biggest challenge we faced was getting the commercial mind-set in place throughout the organization. It probably took us six months to a year to get it drilled into everyone. For some people, it was hard to buy into initially. We heard things like, 'You want me to provide good service, yet you're telling me I can't talk to them [customers] directly anymore?'" But as time went on, Exult's new employees assimilated. "We were loose about some things in the first few months," he said. "Then slowly we started changing things a little at a time. For example, where a voice mail message might have said, 'This is Joe X, please leave a message,' now it would say, 'This is Joe X. If you have an issue with accounts payable, please contact the appropriate help line . . .' and it would list the numbers to call."

Ultimately, Moore says, the new Exult employees and their bank customers came to like the new system because they realized that the service delivery was much more consistent. And for the new Exult employees, there was a big boost when Exult signed Prudential as a client in June 2002, and the call center was suddenly handling more than the Bank of America.

"People's attitudes just skyrocketed then because we saw proof that the business model worked. We were multiclient in one center, and that was a source of pride," Moore said. He added that the transition was also probably easier for Prudential employees than it had been for the bank because the Prudential people didn't already know the Exult staff "from before." "No one at Prudential could say, 'But I used to just call Mary, and she would fix it,'" Moore says. "They didn't know the individuals who were performing the work, so it was easier for them to accept the new system as 'the way we're going to be doing things now.'"

The Bank of America's benefits and payroll functions were moved to Exult by the end of February 2001, and a new call center followed in May. Ramping up the call center was a significant milestone for Exult because it involved handling a high volume of calls and the call center was a start-up staffed with mostly new employees.

Over the summer of 2001, the bank signed an extension of its contract with Exult that called for Exult to take on the administration of expatriate services (services for bank employees moving country to country). In September, the bank signed another extension with Exult, this one calling for Exult to take on the bank's recruiting processes. In that transition, Exult took on an additional 173 former bank employees in a nine-year deal totaling $550 million.

A clear high point in the bank's work with Exult was the merger of the bank's previously separate payroll systems, which took place in April 2002. At the end of 2001, the bank still had two major payrolls—one in Charlotte for about seventy thousand employees and another in Ellinwood, California, which also paid about seventy thousand people. The California payroll was running on Tesseract software; Charlotte was running on PeopleSoft. Exult was handling payroll successfully for the bank from those two locations, but Salvino and Cagle agreed with Steele Alphin that in order for the bank to gain the common platform it wanted, it would be necessary to merge the two systems and handle all payroll from Charlotte.

Bank employees were understandably wary of this change because in 1998, when the bank had attempted to introduce People-Soft in Charlotte, the transition had been fraught with problems. As Salvino recalls, "We had to produce at better than 100 percent because of the challenges the bank had faced the last time it had attempted a payroll conversion." Thus, when the conversion went off seamlessly, both sides saw it as a major victory.

Another high point was the launch of the employee portal in 2003. Among other things, associates at the bank gained computer access to information regarding holiday schedules, benefits, communications, bank news, and open positions. They could view and update personal information, such as home addresses and emergency contacts; view statements of earnings; view or update direct deposit information; and participate in benefits open enrollment, including viewing and editing information about their health care providers and retirement plans. Managers gained access to content that is specific to their individual roles, such as data regarding new employees, leaves of absence, and company events. They also gained access to and the ability to edit information concerning reporting relationships, hiring, transferring, and promotions for direct reports.

Bank of America's $47 billion acquisition of FleetBoston Financial, which was completed in April 2004, has resulted in some significant changes to the bank's HR BPO arrangement. A few weeks after the acquisition, the bank asked Exult to expand its recruiting, temporary staffing, accounts payable, travel and expense, fixed assets, and associated IT support services to the merged entity later in the year. Meanwhile, FleetBoston's benefits and payroll provider, Fidelity, was asked to supply benefits and payroll services to the entire Bank of America organization beginning in 2005. This moves benefits from Hewitt and Mellon, the current providers, and payroll from Exult, the current provider.

The Working Relationship

By December 2001, the Exult–Bank of America team had solidified a way of working together that has become the base model for Exult's future client relationships. The style was set by Cagle (who was leading the relationship from the bank's side) and Salvino (her counterpart at Exult). The two spent a lot of time talking about how they wanted the teams from both companies to behave. They focused on how the relationship was going to evolve and be managed. Today, they can look back and say that what they were in fact trying to do was to create an effective culture for the relationship. But at the time, they didn't use the word *culture*. They just knew that they were in agreement about what kinds of things were going to make or break the undertaking, and that first and foremost among those things was the way in which the teams were going to behave toward one another.

Among other things, they answered the following questions: What will happen when things go wrong? Who will be responsible?

How will conflicts be resolved? How will information travel? How will they ensure open channels of communication? How important are people's titles? Should they deemphasize titles in favor of communication?

Salvino says that one of the ways he could tell if things were working well was if people were simply willing to pitch in, regardless of title, to get a job done. Cagle agrees but also emphasizes that the operation was not free-form, in any sense of the word: "There was a discipline for how teams were set up for each function and for the relationship overall. Within that discipline, there was a lot of freedom."

For example, the operational team members—the group responsible for the day-to-day processes—were, as Cagle says, "hip to hip every day." The members of the account team were responsible for the overall success of the relationship but not necessarily in day-to-day contact. The members of the extended leadership team, which included data security people and audit people, were not involved in a day-to-day sense either, but their accessibility and involvement was no less critical.

"One angry data security person can shut you down if they feel there is a data security risk," Cagle says. "So if there is a question or concern, you need to involve every relevant party as early on as possible, or you'll end up with a firestorm instead of an issue that was resolved before it became a difficult situation. It was and is very important to bring in the extended team early, because if they know what's going on, they can help. But if they don't know what's going on, they will throw up all sorts of barriers in reacting to perceived problems."

For their part, Salvino and Cagle met each day, sometimes briefly, to check in with one another and see how things were. Sometimes that meeting was like being in the eye of a storm. Sometimes the two had been together much of the day anyway, and the meeting seemed redundant. Always, it gave them a deliberate opportunity to shift perspectives, regroup, and remember their senses of humor if the day had been difficult.

Cagle and Salvino also met quarterly with the executive sponsorship team (Oken, Alphin, and another senior representative from the bank, plus Campbell and another senior representative from Exult), and quarterly with Steven Dent, an executive coach, to look at the progress they had made. At those meetings, they asked each other about the big picture. Were they staying true to the commitments they'd made? Was the progress what they'd expected? Were there any unresolved issues regarding the relationship at large? Salvino called those meetings "hard and easy at the same time"—hard because they had to be willing to talk about conflicts and mistakes and easy because they knew that the meetings were in place to help them achieve mutual goals. Salvino recalls:

> There was always something more pressing to do, come those quarterly meetings. But I think we both felt the investment of time was worth it when the meetings were over.
>
> So many times when you're in a high-exposure situation, if something goes wrong, one party will try to put a spin on things that makes them look positive and you look poor. They go into some sort of personal survival mode, and they forget the alliance. Mary Lou put the alliance first all the time, and that's a critical reason why the Bank of America deal worked for them and for us.

Cagle put it this way: "The term 'win-win' is so overused that people don't pay attention to it anymore. But in any situation, when you have a system to refine or an issue to resolve, you're going to end up with either two winners or two losers. And I think that understanding and emphasizing that fact causes Exult and its clients to look for the winning solutions."

Both Cagle and Salvino, along with the other managers from Exult and the bank, emphasize the importance of relying on fact, rather than on impression, in an HR BPO relationship. "Think about it," Cagle says. "When you're handling HR operations for some 150,000 people, something is going to happen every day. The important thing is having the facts of the matter before you start talking, before you start reacting."

In 2001, for example, there were some glitches in the bank's annual benefits enrollment event: changes to the programs were not communicated as clearly as they should have been, and that drove a large number of telephone calls. The call center was staffed leanly, and when the deluge hit, they were overwhelmed. But as Cagle explains, no fingers were pointed, in large part due to the like-minded approach on both sides: "We know what happened; let's get on with it, and note it so that it doesn't happen again."

A low point in the bank's relationship with Exult came when the Charlotte center, in the words of one manager, "started getting balled up because each functional area—payroll, contact center, accounts payable—started running too much like silos. They were good at gaining efficiencies within each function, but that meant redundancy and inefficiency across the boundaries. It wasn't being managed end-to-end, and that's what needed to happen."

As Bob Gunn recalls, "We had to come to grips with the issue because we kept seeing hand-off issues. Information that was needed across the board was being passed along too late. It was a systemic issue, and people were getting out of rapport with one another because of it."

To solve the problem, the two companies held a "summit meeting." Facilitated by Gunn via a Webcast, the operational group came together to talk about the problems and create an action plan for how the various functions would share information going forward. According to Gunn:

> Fundamentally, we had to remind people of their human dimension. We had to help them all recognize that everyone was trying to do the best job they could. The reason you have an organization is that the job at hand is bigger than one person. So to do it requires a collective effort. It requires people to stop listening to the chatter in their own heads. When people are trapped in their own thinking, they come to the table with *my* answers from *my* perspective. And that doesn't get the job done. But when you clear that chatter, people suddenly start to connect, and it feels good. And the moment that people rise above their personal issues, the tone in the room

lifts, and they start seeing the bigger picture. The moment they can see the broader issues, they start having productive insights.

Results

In addition to delivering the cost savings agreed to in the contract, Exult's work has helped the bank do the following:

- Manage the cost-service mix it wishes to deliver to its associates. Performance targets and cost-to-serve standards are set; they are no longer by-products of the processes. For example, days-to-hire used to be measured as the outcome of the process. Today, it's an input in the Exult service delivery model (the bank wants it to be fewer than forty days), and it is measured and tracked to make sure the bank gets the results it wants to. (In early 2004, the figure was fewer than thirty-four days.)

- Pay more attention to designing the service offering it wants to deliver, with the confidence that the back office partners can deliver. For example, in 2002, in response to the rising costs of providing health care, the bank radically revised its health care strategy, which involved massive changes for providers, coverages, coverage areas, employee participation costs, and so forth. Exult worked with the bank to design how the changes would be communicated to associates and helped deliver on a flawless enrollment execution involving more than eighty thousand active enrollments, with 95 percent of those handled through automated channels.

- Make systemic, fact-based improvements to the processes that serve its employees. For example, before Exult, escalations related to personnel services were fielded and worked one by one. The effort to address each issue was significant and left little time to determine if there was a common theme that needed to be addressed. Working with the bank, Exult developed an "escalation response team" that not only addresses each issue, but also logs and tracks root causes, providing the information needed to identify trends and stop problems from recurring.

Another example of systemic improvements is the bank's adaptation of Six Sigma methodology. Exult has collaborated with the bank on the development of multiple end-to-end Six Sigma process improvement initiatives (such as the bank's leave-of-absence process). Exult also provides the transaction-level data needed to identify and address improvement opportunities across HR processes.

• Focus energy on the issues that matter most to the bank's core business. For example, in 2002, HR personnel rolled out a corporation-wide "Spirit" program focused on ensuring the quality of the customer experience, redesigned and implemented the new health care strategy mentioned previously, and changed its approach to compensation.

• Marshal the resources needed to address changes in the personnel infrastructure, including a conversion from Tesseract to PeopleSoft, consolidating two major processing operations (Ellinwood with Charlotte).

• Begin the movement of Bank of America HR on to a Web-based self-service system. The bank has rolled out a state-of-the-art recruiting platform (Employ!), installed an advanced compensation planning tool from Kadiri, implemented a new platform for managing global assignees (Global Advantage), and established the foundation portal for much greater employee and manager Web-enabled self-service. The bank has begun a two-year effort that, when completed, will provide all associates with access to the Bank of America associates' portal.

Learnings and Conclusions

Many of the faces have changed since the initial contract between Exult and the bank was signed. The job of managing the relationship from the bank's side, for example, has changed hands four times since the contract was signed. Much has changed, too, in terms of the level of sophistication at the bank and at Exult regarding HR outsourcing arrangements, particularly with respect to measurements and metrics. "From activity measurements to performance measurements, you can really look at the original contract and say we're all a lot smarter now, after three years," says Anthony Marino, who currently heads the relationship from the bank's side. "A lot of that knowledge has come through implementing Six Sigma. But we also have a better understanding of where to look for improvement, and how to gauge our measurements."

As Marino sees it, "Clearly we would have made the same decision to outsource today as we did back then. A company can reduce costs in this space by 20 to 25 percent by having someone else do the kind of work that an HR outsourcing provider does. But today, if I were advising other companies going into an HR outsourcing contract, I would say they should look not only at costs but be as diligent about the productivity improvement side of things." It's easier today, Marino notes, to be more specific about expectations regarding productivity gains, because the industry as a whole is more knowledgeable about what to measure and how.

As Bank of America has become more disciplined in its approach to process improvement through the use of Six Sigma tools, the demands on all of its suppliers have intensified. For example, the key performance indicators used to measure Exult's performance are evolving to become more quality driven versus activity driven. Another example is how the answer rate, which measures how fast Exult's representatives answer the phone, is evolving to include a new primary metric called first call resolution. It measures if an associate received the help he or she needed. A third example is payroll accuracy, which started out measuring only Exult's processing accuracy, but has evolved. Today, the measure looks at payroll accuracy end-to-end. "Associates don't care who made a mistake; they know that there is an error in their paycheck, resulting in a poor associate experience," Marino explains. "By viewing business processes like payroll in an end-to-end fashion, as we're doing now, the bank and Exult can work jointly to fix a root cause issue, lower transaction costs, and improve associate experience. All these changes in how performance is measured will take the relationship to an even better place for both companies."

Marino recommends that companies considering HR outsourcing study thoroughly what is going to go on the Web, when, and how—in advance of signing a contract. "If you want to build an integrated environment, where redundancies don't occur through the use of the Web, you need to do that," he says. "Many companies have ended up doing what we're doing—ditching a lot of redundant applications. But people can do it right the first time now by learning through the mistakes of the first movers. The climate has changed in the past three years. Three years ago, there wasn't a lot of demand for Web-enabled tools like e-performance management or compensation planning systems; today there is."

Additional productivity and efficiency can be gained by moving transactions from more expensive channels like call centers to the Web. But this can be tricky for both the company and the HR BPO provider. Because of this Marino says providing associates with a choice between telephone and the Web will always be a part of Bank of America's strategy.

Self-service tools and applications that are Web enabled and support business processes can result in an overly complicated delivery model. Their integration needs to be carefully thought out from a manager and associate perspective; otherwise, the user experience may not be a satisfactory one. An example is the bank's talent planning process. Marino says that three Web tools support different steps in the talent planning process, and some require duplication of information. Solving this type of problems will require a much higher level of integration between the various HR processes and applications.

Finally, Marino notes, it is increasingly important for companies using HR outsourcing providers to understand—and influence—what work will be done in the United States and what will be done abroad. "If your outsourcer wants to put the call center in India, you want to be able to have a point of view on that," he says. "You want to be able to choose on the basis of price and value. Exult did outsource our call center to India, and it has been a challenge regarding our associates' experiences with that center. Exult is being very responsive, and the situation is improving, but this is something that I'd suggest other companies move carefully with."

The bank remains committed to the HR BPO approach now that it has acquired FleetBoston, but with an important difference: it will have two vendors instead of one. Among the challenges going forward will be continuing the aggressive plans in the HR function that were approved before the merger, such as offering mutual fund options to associates and installing a new timekeeping system. It will also need to consolidate the Bank of America and Fleet HR processes and programs and move everyone to a common technology platform. This will have to be done while a new vendor, Fidelity, takes over several key processes. Adding a second major HR BPO vendor is likely to create complexity for Bank of America. Key to the success of Bank of America's new approach to HR BPO will be the development of a good working relationship among the bank, Exult, and Fidelity.

Chapter Eight

International Paper

Business: Paper/packaging and forest products

Contract signing: October 2001

Contract term: Ten years

Contract value: $600 million initially; contract grew by
approximately $90 million during the first year

Geographical coverage: United States

Employees in company: Approximately 90,000 at contract signing

Employees covered: Approximately 53,000 active employees and
60,000 retirees or term vested

Scope: HR administration, excluding recruiting, training, and
selection

In early 1993, the HR executives in International Paper (IP) decided to focus on how they could improve the department's performance. They had been busy, in recent years, as a result of acquisitions and growth. IP had acquired the HammerMill Paper Company in 1986 in a $1.1 billion transaction. The company had also gone global in the late 1980s and early 1990s, acquiring two European paper companies and a majority shareholder interest in Carter Holt Harvey of New Zealand, among other initiatives. Sales were on an unprecedented upward trend, and the HR function was struggling to manage the diverse processes of the fast-growing entity.

The HR department had recently outsourced health and welfare administration, savings plan administration, pension administration, and relocation administration. HR was handling payroll for more than 200 locations, managing more than 120 union contracts, and administrating more than 400 benefit plan combinations, totaling more than 72,000 benefit rates. There were more than 800 earnings codes, over 1,300 payroll deduction codes, and more than 130 interfaces and file feeds with third-party providers. The department was running outdated systems, and there was no employee self-service or electronically enabled technology in use.

There was a clear need to standardize processes and procedures. Managers in HR felt that by standardizing and improving their processes, they could significantly reduce their departments' operating costs.

HR leader Paul Karre, a twenty-eight-year veteran of the company, and his colleagues were aware of the literature about the potential of HR departments to pull back from administration and engage in company strategy. They had a long-term vision of what the department could contribute to the company. But they were also realists and understood that a transformation of the department at the time was too difficult a goal. So they decided to focus their initial efforts on standardizing payroll across the company. With top management approval and investment, they committed to building a centralized employee service center and purchased Empower, which they felt was the latest, most promising software technology at the time.

It was, in Karre's words, "a disaster." "The problems were immediate and numerous," he recalls. "And they couldn't be fixed." The software that the company deployed was not ready; it was a pre-beta version. Moreover, IP lacked the proper IT infrastructure to run an integrated system across the entire company. In addition, IP had not attempted to simplify its existing processes before the transition to the new framework. IP had also reduced the number of people on its HR staff before changing its processes, resulting in fewer people running a slew of systems without the kind of safety net that a staff with a wealth of experience can provide.

"I think we made every mistake that could have been made," Karre says. "We were trying to cut costs, and we did, but we did not get the results we had hoped for. Long story short, we pulled the plug in 1997."

HR did elect to keep its employee service center. However, the center operated the older legacy technology and reverted back to using its older processes. Needless to say, the failed change initiative left HR with a tarnished image. Within the department, morale was low, and there was little, if any, further talk about how HR could transform itself. Instead, managers kept their heads down and fought a daily, seemingly endless, battle with paperwork.

Then, in 1999, IP merged with Union Camp. As part of the merger agreement, Jerry Carter of Union Camp was named senior vice president of HR, and he brought with him new resolve and a tremendous amount of energy. He felt strongly that HR needed a complete overhaul and immediately became the champion of a change effort.

One of the first things Carter did was to regroup the leadership in HR and engage them in what he called an "opportunity assessment." He resurrected the long-term vision of HR as a strategic contributor to the company and charged the group to think about exactly what HR needed to accomplish in order to get out of the business of administration and move into a more strategic role.

At first, this group had a hard time identifying what they wanted to provide because they didn't fully understand what their line managers needed or wanted (or could envision wanting) from the HR department. Carter's solution was to have IP's senior HR managers spend a great deal of time with the business leaders in the company exploring "What do you need from HR and what if HR could do this for you?" scenarios, and also attempting, for the first time, to understand strategically where the company was going.

"It was out of that effort that we developed our 'real' transformation strategy," Karre says. "And once we knew it was real, we let the entire organization know as well." They also gave the initiative a name, Project Viking, which within the group had some significance. "We actually came up with the name when we were sitting around the kitchen table at one of the manager's homes one night, and he had just bought a Viking stove," Karre says. "But we also remembered our history. The Vikings burned their ships when they reached a foreign land so that they couldn't go back, even if they wanted to. We liked the idea of sending a message to the company that we were going to get it right this time, and we weren't going to turn back."

The effort the department put into promoting Project Viking was an important part of the transformation that was to come. The senior HR managers had learned a great deal from their earlier failure, not the least of which was that a transformation effort on the scale and scope they were proposing had to start with some deconstruction. "We had learned," recalls Karre, "that technology will do anything you program it to do, but the last thing we wanted to do was to deploy new technology to run our old processes."

Themes for Change

Eight strategic themes emerged from the discussions the HR managers had with IP's senior line managers and the analysis the HR department did as a result of those talks. Four were focused on the internal workings of the HR department. What could HR do for HR? The other four were focused on what HR could do for International Paper.

The internal change themes for HR were: aligning HR with the business, enhancing HR capabilities, executing the service delivery model, and measuring HR performance. The HR for IP themes were: developing leaders, developing people, building customer-focus capabilities ("customer" meaning the customers of the HR department—that is, IP's employees), and enhancing change management capabilities.

Broadly, these themes reflected a strategic shift in the company from being asset focused to customer focused. As Karre says,

> This is a capital-intensive industry, and in the old days, you optimized your tangible assets and that's all you needed to do. But in the competitive climate of the late 1990s, leveraging capital became the ante companies needed to stay in the game. We have tremendous threats to our business from product substitution such as plastics and from offshore competitors in terms of costs. And we wanted our HR leaders to be working with business leaders to redesign work to change behaviors, help employees better understand their roles, develop the kinds of leaders who can move the company forward. We didn't want them any longer to be making sure that someone's address was correct in the system.

In other words, the themes pointed to an HR department that identified administration as a baseline capability and was able to add value to the company in other ways.

Getting Administration Under Control

Taken as a whole, the eight themes—and the myriad of possible actions those themes suggested—might have overwhelmed the department. Often when a change effort of such magnitude is begun, the vision is so vague and hopeful that it eschews real-life limits. But with the memories of the department's payroll failure fresh, Carter and his leadership team were particularly careful to set realistic expectations and approach the task in a practical way. To that end, they decided to look at the department from a supply-and-demand point of view and frame their goals in terms of three levels of success:

Level One: Getting the administrative end of HR under control, reducing costs substantively, and improving service-delivery.

Level Two: Aligning HR more closely with the strategic goals of the business, and finding a way for HR to contribute in a significant way to leadership development.

Level Three: A long-term goal—the total transformation of the HR department into a function that could drive business model development for the company by guiding the deployment of its professionals and supplying relevant organizational design expertise.

One of the first steps toward gaining control of the department's administrative tasks was the decision to purchase the SAP platform for payroll. At this time, IP was running five source systems: standard payroll, Lawson, JD Edwards, Tesseract, and "pension manager," a third-party system for retirees.

The company converted the salaried population to SAP in early 2001 and immediately started reaping the benefits of the move in terms of cost reduction and increased efficiencies. However, Karre and his colleagues realized that the momentum of that success would soon be lost if the department did not make other improvements. Cost-reduction levels would soon plateau unless the company could find a way to gain economies of scale.

That is where Exult entered the picture. "Our focus up until then had been, 'How do we do this?'" Karre explains. "But at that point, we started thinking more along the lines of, "How do we do this better?'"

Exult was not a stranger to IP. In fact, it would be more accurate to say that Exult reentered the picture, because the company had initially approached IP in 1999 to gauge its interest in becoming an Exult customer. Carter and his team had politely begged off then on the grounds that they were just getting their own house in order. But now the timing seemed right, and when Exult again contacted IP, they were ready to talk. As Mark Azzarello, director of HR operations for IP, reflects, IP probably would not have contacted Exult on its own; more likely, IP would have completed the Viking conversion and then given some thought to outsourcing. But when

Exult made contact again, IP managers realized the time was right for a deal with Exult.

"We wanted to be contractually committed to service levels with predictable scaling and guaranteed cost reduction over the term of the contract," Karre explains. "Exult could do that for us because this work is their core competency, and they had the scale. We couldn't do it by ourselves; we didn't have the size. But when we looked at Exult and added in the population from Bank of America, we realized that they had enough scale to push the costs down much further than we could."

Azzarello concurs: "Our plan really focused on our function, and moving it toward the value-added activities and away from the administration. Benefits and payroll administration is not our core competency. So we wanted to look for a company for which that kind of administration is a core competency. When we installed SAP, it had been twenty-five years since our last HR upgrade. Left to our own devices, we also knew that it would probably be a long time before we could do it again. Exult, on the other hand, was obligated to improve continually. We believed we'd be able to stay on the cutting edge of HR processes through them."

Exult, for its part, looked at IP and saw (as it had back in 1999) both a Fortune 50 client and access to the SAP platform. Exult felt it was important to add experience with an SAP installation to its portfolio of offerings because it is such a widely used ERP software. It also saw a service center that was ripe for acquisition.

"We had our house in order," Azzarello notes. "So I don't think we would be Exult's prototypical target. But we also had SAP, which Exult wanted, and we presented an opportunity for the company to acquire another strength."

Azzarello says that the company expected that Exult would redesign certain processes over time in order to achieve the synergies needed to gain economies of scale. But the IP managers knew that Exult would be starting way ahead of where they started with most clients because they would be acquiring some state-of-the-art processes.

Carter, Karre, and Azzarello visited Exult in Houston in June 2001, initiating a series of discussions that culminated in an agreement to enter into a due diligence process. "We thought it would be a thirty-day process," Azzarello notes, "but it took a full ninety days, in large part because Exult was still such a new company and we wanted to vet it thoroughly. It was important for both organizations to conduct a full business case analysis to ensure that entering into an agreement was the right thing to do."

The two companies negotiated a deal that IP brought to its board at the beginning of the fourth quarter of 2001. A ten-year, $600 million contract was signed calling for Exult to begin work in January 2002.

"It was the most complex agreement I had ever been involved in," Azzarello notes. In part, that was because the deal was structured so that IP would get due credit for the initiatives it had already begun. The two parties had to agree on an appropriate time for Exult to begin to deliver cost savings and get credit for those savings.

Another complication centered on gain-sharing. During negotiations, IP's managers found themselves asking questions about gain-sharing possibilities that Exult at the time wasn't able to answer because it had little relevant experience. This wasn't considered a negative by either side, but it did add another layer of complexity to the negotiation process. The two parties decided to put together a gain-sharing governance committee to study the issue jointly.

From a distance, gain-sharing seems fairly straightforward. As it has worked out in IP's case, the company has taken third-party providers—health care providers, temporary labor, relocation providers—and either assigned that relationship to Exult or asked Exult to manage the relationship. If there was a fiduciary relationship, IP has maintained ownership of the contract. Exult has managed the relationship and the vendor's performance for a fee. If there was no fiduciary relationship, then IP has assigned the provider to Exult, and Exult has the right to change providers so long as it delivers the same services at reduced costs. When costs are reduced, Exult and IP share the cost savings.

The vendor arrangements ended up being complex and varied. Some vendors had long-term relationships with International Paper and were leery of having their contract assigned to a third party. In some cases, the issue was one of finances: some vendors were looking for financial protection from International Paper, rather than the start-up company, Exult.

The final HR BPO contract had several major components. It called for Exult to take on IP's service center and service center staff. This involved two hundred people based in Memphis, occupying sixty-three thousand square feet of leased space that Exult would sublease from IP. Exult also took on the employees in IP's HR information management department, approximately forty people based in the same locale as the service center employees.

As far as processes go, the deal included benefits administration, payroll administration, third-party (vendor) administration, health and welfare administration, relocation services, the employee assistance program, and drug testing. IP's HR department retained responsibility and operational control of administration surrounding corporate compensation activities (such as stock option administration), expatriate administration, and salary forecasting. IP also retained the administrative duties involving recruiting, talent selection, and training.

"I think it's key to note that we viewed the arrangement as a divestiture of sorts," Azzarello says. "Other Exult clients may not approach the deal in that way, but that was what we wanted. A transaction took place, and we did not take an equity position in Exult. We elected not to take warrants or options; we elected to execute a cash transaction."

The transaction was not a simple divestiture, however. Both companies had to invest a lot of management time to ensure that the transition went smoothly because in an important way, changing the name on the door of the service center from International Paper to Exult was both an end and an important beginning.

IP never seriously considered other possible providers, though it did a thorough reference check on Exult. But IP never seriously considered other vendors. Karre says this was because no other provider at the time was offering a full spectrum of services; Azzarello also notes that Exult was the only pure-play provider able to handle IP's processes end-to-end.

Both Karre and Azzarello say that they are satisfied with the way things turned out. But both also would advise other HR departments to cast a wider net in their own searches. "Times have changed," Karre says. "We were exploring our options just as the HR BPO industry was forming."

Transitioning

Azzarello notes that Exult had begun "putting some resources on the ground" even as the contract negotiations were nearing completion, so as to be ready when it was signed. But even so, the elapsed time from the contract signing and announcement to the actual transition of employees and facility from IP to Exult was only ten weeks.

During the ten weeks, IP did not communicate a great deal about the change to the general workforce. "IP's communications to the organization at large were passive," Azzarello says. "We didn't want to make a big issue of the transition and leave an impression that if something went wrong, it was Exult's responsibility. The only thing that changed January first was the name on the door as far as our employees were concerned. The people at the service center hadn't changed. The processes hadn't changed. So we simply communicated the decision that the company had made in a low-key way."

The opposite was true of IP's approach to the company's leadership. HR managers did a great deal of communicating with senior company managers to ensure that they understood the economic rationale behind the decision. For example, they made the economics of the deal as transparent as possible, providing reports on the cost of service levels before Exult and the expected savings down the road. They also made HR strategy as transparent as possible, detailing for senior IP managers and line managers their short- and long-term goals. Where possible, they tried to make explicit connections between what they were doing and what they had learned from these same managers during their initial fact-finding missions. This enabled managers to see how their needs were going to be addressed.

IP's HR managers and their counterparts at Exult were also extremely conscientious about communicating often and clearly with the employees who were moving from IP to Exult. With this group, both companies worked hard to keep the channels of communication open in order to defray and alleviate any concerns they had about becoming Exult employees.

The IP employees who were moving to Exult fell into three distinct categories. First, there were those who were either new to the company or weren't greatly concerned with who their employer was as long as they were paid. This was the smallest group but nonetheless recognizable. Exult and IP together found that the transition for this group was easy. The companies made several formal announcements, offered question-and-answer sessions, and developed transition activities including informational meetings, various Exult new employee orientation activities, and an event marking the closing of an era with IP. They found that little else was needed.

The second category was made up of individuals who saw themselves as service center employees. Recognizing that the company they were moving to was going to provide them an environment in which service center operations were the core competency and a profit center, these people were optimistic and enthusiastic. The dot-com bubble hadn't yet burst, which also helped matters with this group. They weren't instinctively wary of any new company touting Web enablement. Exult and IP used the same approach with this group as they did with those in the first category: they provided the facts of the transition, and they made it clear that they were open to questions. They found that this group, too, needed little more in the way of hand-holding.

In the third category were individuals who saw themselves either as IP employees or as HR professionals who happened to be working in the service center on their way up the management ladder. It is not uncommon in the paper industry to find people with twenty-five or thirty years of experience with a single employer, and there were many in this group. These people were hard hit by the move. They were wary of Exult, angry with IP, and understandably nervous about their futures. Julie MacDonald, Stacey Cadigan, and Cliff Sass of Exult worked closely with this group, many of whom were tapped for leadership roles in the transition process and have benefited from the change. The Memphis center added a second client in August 2003 and is poised to take on additional client volume. This has afforded new career growth and development opportunities to the former IP employees who now work for Exult.

It has been a different story for the IP IT staff. Outsourcing was not an IT decision. The IT staff had operated in a culture that saw HR as their customer. The HR IT functions were integrally linked to the HR processes, which made the transfer of this area to Exult very important. Exult supports IT through a global delivery model, which resulted in a different set of dynamics for the IT staff as compared to employees in HR. Some IT employees transferred to Exult, but many elected to remain with IP and were redeployed to other initiatives. For all the employees moving to Exult, the emphasis was on the greater career potential associated with moving to a company whose core business was HR BPO.

"I give Exult a tremendous amount of credit for the integration activities they put in place and for the way they engaged the people moving to Exult," Azzarello says. "They had a series of teams made up of people on both sides responsible for different phases of the transition, and they tried to keep everyone informed and upbeat as we passed the torch. For example, I used to conduct a quarterly informational meeting off-site with the entire service center staff. During the fourth quarter meeting in 2001, Exult ran that meeting, and they used it as an opportunity to start a new chapter. They made it clear that they were open to fielding any questions anyone wanted to serve up."

"It didn't help matters that the service center had to work on January 1, 2002," Azzarello reflects. "New Year's Day happened to be a payroll day, and the center was open for business. So the people who moved from IP to Exult got started working on a holiday."

Results

At this writing, IP is over two years into its contract with Exult. There have been many successes but also some bumps in the road, as one would expect in any new relationship. Proof of the arrangement's success comes first in the numbers. As Karre says, "You will find us to be extremely metric conscious, these days, in HR. We measure a lot. Some people would think we measure ad nauseam. . . . But we understand the value of facts in keeping our transformation underway."

- In 1998, at the time Karre and his fellow HR managers were building the business case for Project Viking, there were 675 employees in the HR department, serving 54,000 active employees, or 1 HR person for every 80 employees. As of 2003, the company had 400 HR staffers serving approximately 53,000 employees, or 1 HR person for every 133 employees.
- The financial data are compelling. In 1998, Karre says IP was spending approximately $1,600 per employee serviced annually. By comparison, the budget for 2004 calls for HR to spend about $1,149 per employee. This shift of more than $400 per person, translates into some $24 million a year for IP.
- Employee self-service capabilities currently include essential administrative transactions such as change of address, emergency contact information, and W-4 changes. In addition, all open enrollment activity, pension administration, and savings plan administration activities are available through employee self-service. The

current penetration rate for self-service transactions is approximately 65 percent, with a target of 70 percent by mid-2004. Also by mid-2004, IP expects to complete an upgrade of its portal, which will significantly expand employee self-service transaction capabilities. Changes in life activities, such as the addition and deletion of dependents, benefits enrollment, and new employee orientation will be available.

• What of IP's commitment to achieving three distinct levels of success with regard to transforming its HR department? The department has achieved its Level One aspirations. The goal (successfully met) was to have all of the domestic staff on SAP by the middle of 2003. Costs are down markedly, as noted, and the ten-year projections for cost reduction and improved efficiencies are on track.

Level Two goals also seem to be well in hand. HR managers feel that their efforts to reduce costs, along with their increasing knowledge about their employee base, has helped them contribute more value to the organization than they had in the past.

Level Three has not been achieved. HR is not yet active in business development, but it is starting to happen. "We're clearly doing it," Karre says. "In 1998, we were at the lower end of the first level, and today I think you'd find that we're at the high end of Level Two, and in some areas, even the low end of Level Three. In fact, if you were to ask the company's senior leadership if they have seen a positive change in the function and in the function's impact on the business, without hesitation you would get a resounding yes.

Some IP managers, however, question whether the Exult contract has substantively contributed to the company's achieving those goals. They point to the fact that IP had already decided to reinvent the HR department before Exult came on the scene. Still, there is little question that Exult has produced cost savings and that IP now has data that it never had before, data that can be used to help HR reach Level Three.

Lessons Learned

IP's managers can say with some justifiable pride that if they were starting over and initiating talks with Exult tomorrow, there isn't a lot they would change in terms of the way they set up the deal. But that is not to say that the company didn't learn some valuable lessons that will guide their actions in the future.

For example, they learned the value of knowing their own cost structure thoroughly before entering into the process. As Azzarello says, "Typically, an outsourcer will say there's a cost benefit to the deal. But too many people enter into negotiations without really knowing if that's the case." IP knew what its service center cost structure was. The company had sound baselines to use as reference points, so when Exult put its business case, with ten-year projections, on the table, IP managers were able to determine immediately whether it was viable and reasonable.

But in other areas, they weren't as prepared. In order to deal with three of these areas, the two companies did due diligence on expatriate administration, stock options, and salary forecasting. But as Azzarello says, "We didn't know what those three areas cost us to run. So we had to bring in our internal audit department to do some analysis and figure out what our baseline costs were and would be. It would have helped to have had that information in hand prior to initiating discussions about those areas with Exult."

Another lesson IP took away from its deal with Exult was the importance of clear communication regarding the details of the contract. "Every time you look at adding something on, you should go through a mini-due-diligence," Azzarello says. "Is this extra, 'out-of-scope' service reflective of what you really want? Are the expectations clearly understood? Could you do it yourself for less?"

Exult and IP managers agree that expectations are often easily misunderstood; both emphasize the importance of thorough communication about even the smallest add-ons to avoid misconceptions. "Here's an example," Azzarello says. "We recently completed our open enrollment process. It's a standard process within the baseline cost structure, but because of some unusual circumstances this year involving a medical provider, we had to open up our enrollment period for an additional week. We were talking with Exult about doing it, and the first price quote that came in was exorbitant. The reason, as I found out, was that they didn't quite understand what I was looking for. We have open lines of communication, so I was able to quickly go back and clarify things. But I can see that in another relationship, this sort of thing could have gotten out of hand rapidly."

A third lesson IP managers took away from their work with Exult is the importance of being involved in the process of developing solutions. Karre cites the two companies' experience with formulating the gain-sharing deal as a good example of this lesson, and Azzarello concurs. "Never assume that the outsourcer knows everything," he says. "And this has nothing to do with trust; it's just good problem solving. Don't assume that if the outsourcer suggests an approach to something, it is automatically suggesting the best option. It is possible that you know something the outsourcer doesn't— about the issue at hand, about your business."

Lesson four is to stay engaged. As IP managers learned, BPO deals must be partnerships. The company outsourcing the work has to stay involved in a day-to-day relationship with the outsourcer to ensure that the work unfolds in a way that meets expectations on both sides. "Your expectations are also going to change naturally as you progress," Azzarello says. "New opportunities are going to arise, and you're also going to face some challenges you hadn't anticipated. So you want to make sure that your providers' expectations are in line with your own."

Good governance is critical to the success of a BPO arrangement. In IP's case, the company has a steering committee made up of officers from both companies, as well as the relationship managers. The relationship managers meet weekly to review the overall relationship and strategic issues. A larger meeting is held monthly to discuss operational governance. This meeting typically includes the relationship managers along with those involved operationally from

HR, IT, and other areas outsourced to Exult. The format of the meeting usually focuses on discussing significant operational issues, changes that need to be made, and action items that need addressing. This meeting is much more tactical than strategic in nature.

Constant communication is also an integral part of a working partnership. IP managers now know that they can't change anything in HR that doesn't have some kind of an impact on Exult and vice versa. The relationship is not simply "I'm the client; you're the vendor," as it would be in a one-dimensional outsourcing deal. With a payroll vendor, for example, IP could simply expect paychecks to show up on time, and there wouldn't be much to manage in terms of a relationship. With Exult, so many services are entwined in the deal that managing the relationship is crucial.

For example, when IP's HR department identified the need for a companywide time-entry system, it decided to put a pilot system in place, but quickly ran into a funding problem for the pilot (competing, as it was, for resources with other parts of the company). IP's managers talked with Exult about the issue, and Exult is now funding and managing the pilot program. The cost will be offset against some of the gain-sharing agreement returns.

As Azzarello notes,

> This is something that could happen only in a partnership. There's something in it for Exult. We're relieving them of some of the burden they had agreed to take on as part of the gain-sharing agreement. And they're also looking for other services they can leverage for other clients, so a time-entry system might fill a need at some point. Exult will have developed an expertise with the system through firsthand experience. But if we didn't have the kind of relationship we have, we never would have thought to raise the issue with them. The pilot would have died, and the idea placed on a back-burner until we could garner the resources.

Finally, IP and Exult managers alike stress the ongoing importance of fact-based decisions, fact-based assessments of process, and setting clear deadlines regarding performance improvements and change. These may be basic principles of business, but all too often, fundamental standards like these can get lost in the throes of day-to-day detail. "It's easy to lose sight of where you are because there are so many things to keep track of. We've all done it," Azzarello says. "But you have to keep in mind that if there weren't a reasonable business reason to set a deadline, you wouldn't have set it in the first place. It's important to hold people accountable on both sides, because once you start to slip, it's hard to regain your traction."

Future Directions

Now the challenge is to ensure that the IP organization as a whole accepts the HR function's new role. Too often, when a department emerges successfully from a major transformation effort, there is a brief honeymoon, and then the momentum of the change effort is lost. Old habits resurface, old procedures are rediscovered ("well, just this once, because I know it will be faster if I do it the old way . . ."), and progress erodes.

As Karre recounts, "I was in Wisconsin just recently with a group of HR leaders, and one of them was saying to me that it would be great if they had access to the employee data that the reps in the service center see, so that they could look things up when employees had questions. And I said, 'Absolutely not.' The value HR adds is no longer about looking up the status of someone's sickness benefits. If we're going to sustain the sea-change we've seen in the nature of our jobs, we have to reinforce a similar change in employees and line managers' expectations of our jobs."

Put another way, it's easy to say to the company at large that HR is now a business partner, or that the function is now aligned to the business strategy, but what's important is making sure that everyone, from the company's senior management team to the line managers, understands what those words mean in practice. The HR department at IP wants the company's business managers to remember the kinds of things they said back in 1998, when they were articulating "if only . . ." scenarios for how HR could help them. And it wants them to continue to demand those kinds of high-level services, not revert to thinking of HR as a paper mover.

The department's legacy is part of the problem. When Karre joined IP some twenty-nine years ago, HR was the "personnel department." Then it became the "employee relations" department. "A lot of us became very successful because we were good administrators," Karre recalls. "A person would come in with an administrative problem, and I would solve it. I felt good; the employee was satisfied. But those things don't add a lot of value to the business.

"We must remind ourselves," Karre concludes. "There is so much that line managers should expect from this function, and they are beginning to understand that the value of HR is not in administrative management. The real value is when HR leaders are at the table engaged in the debate and helping move the organization and our business forward through people development, employee engagement, diversity, and change leadership."

Chapter Nine

Prudential

Business: Financial services

Contract signing: January 2002

Contract term: Ten years

Size: $700 million

Geographical coverage: United States

Employees in company: 47,000 at contract signing

Employees covered: 31,000

Scope: Comprehensive HR administration, operations, and
technology, excluding relocation and expatriate services; also
accounts payable

"Going back roughly six years before we contracted with Exult, to 1996 or so, it's safe to say that HR at Prudential was not at an optimum place," says Sharon Taylor, senior vice president of corporate human resources at the company. "We were large; we had a great deal of replication. I'd say that we had pockets of excellence here and there in terms of transaction management, but we weren't integrated by any means. We weren't aligned. We couldn't, for example, leverage technology across different parts of the function. And we were aware that down the road, the systems and structures we had in place weren't going to continue working for us."

In 1996 HR at Prudential was getting its work done from the point of view of employees. But the function clearly needed process improvements. Managers on the inside were aware that costs were too high and efficiency was lacking, and both costs and efficiency were on a track to get worse.

Then, in the spring of 1997, Michele Darling left Canadian Imperial Banking Corporation to join Prudential as the head of HR. Darling made it clear to everyone in HR at Prudential that her goal was to root out inefficiencies in staffing and processes. She introduced an initiative that called for a series of strategic consulting engagements in each line of Prudential's business with an eye toward streamlining operations. As Taylor explains, Darling "brought in expertise that the company didn't have inside, to help us assess where we were, what we could do to make things better, and ultimately, to drive much of the change we've experienced."

Over the next three years, Darling's initiatives resulted in some visible improvements in the function. "Many of the problems were corrected," says Taylor. "For example, we centralized staffing and on-campus recruiting and outsourced clerical hiring. We also replaced our former HRIS system with PeopleSoft and introduced a benefits call center for our associates, 1–800-PRU-EASY, that over time, evolved to customer satisfaction ratings in the 90s."

But like many change efforts, this one began to reach a plateau where the improvements were no longer as great as they had been in the beginning. "We hit a point where we knew it was time to step back and take stock," Taylor says. "We had realized some gains, but we needed to figure out how to take the function to the next level. What was the next logical set of actions? What did we need to do so that the structure and the goals of HR could manifest themselves against a backdrop of cost reduction?"

Prudential's HR managers, led by Darling, who also had responsibility for the company's corporate governance functions, started to evaluate HR anew at the end of 2000 while doing business planning for 2001. "In part, that meant looking at everything we did and asking what, why, how, and where," says Taylor. "From there, we concluded that some things had outlived their usefulness and should no longer be done; others needed to be done but, given available technology or business nuances, not by HR. Still other work needed to be handled directly by the businesses."

It also meant taking a hard look at transactional work. Taylor, along with Sekhar Ramaswamy, vice president of process reengineering, and Paul Evans, vice president of HR administrative services, participated in a series of meetings to identify the core work of Prudential's HR department versus the noncore work. Among other things, they asked themselves: What do we want to work on? In what ways do we contribute to the organization as a whole? In what strategic ways do we contribute? How do we add value? Does the value we add justify the cost in each area?

Those questions unleashed a torrent of thinking about the potential of the HR function in general, and in particular at Prudential. The outcome was a reinvigorated philosophy about what HR could offer to the company. It featured strategic value as a consultative business partner and delivery of administrative services at reduced costs.

The core work of the department would be using its knowledge of the professionals within the organization to contribute in a much greater way regarding staffing allocation, Prudential's capabilities, and the company's capacity to take advantage of opportunities in the marketplace. This understanding led them to the question: How do we want to get the noncore-yet-necessary work done? That question prompted them to start modeling different scenarios for what their transformed department would look like.

What-If Scenarios

"That's about where we were at the end of 2000," Taylor says. "We were exploring internal options and were also beginning to consider outsourcing." The department was thorough in its explorations. "We looked at all sorts of internal possibilities," Taylor explains. "We had reached a point of diminishing returns on a number of fronts where we didn't have the scale needed to reduce our delivery cost further. So we ran through several what-if scenarios."

One of the options Prudential considered was building a robust shared-service center in-house, and then going into that business— taking on outside customers—to gain the scale necessary to reduce costs. Prudential also considered moving much of the administrative work of the HR department offshore to a Prudential operation in Ireland. The economics weren't guaranteed in that scenario, but they were attractive. Another option was starting up a business in sourcing people. "We could have assumed that since we had a best practice in sourcing people, we could gain scale by setting up a small business doing that for other companies," Taylor recalls.

Many of the options were viable and even intriguing, given the possibilities they raised for the future of Prudential's HR managers and the department as a whole. But with each new scenario they explored, Darling, Taylor, Ramaswamy, and their colleagues ultimately concluded that going forward would mean a departure from their original goal: adding strategic value to Prudential's core businesses. As Taylor says, "We had to ask ourselves, 'Do we want to develop an expertise in something that is not Prudential's core competency?' The answer was always no."

Outsourcing increasingly seemed to be the best idea. The more deeply Prudential's HR executives researched outsourcing, the more they realized that a BPO arrangement could take the noncore work off their hands and do it as well or better at a lower cost. They believed that if they weren't mired in day-to-day operational tasks, they could mine and use HR data to Prudential's strategic advantage in terms of staffing and organizational effectiveness. They also thought they could reduce costs and increase their strategic contribution to the company exponentially.

"In some organizations," Taylor notes, "outsourcing can be like the bubonic plague. It takes everything away and leaves nothing behind. You outsource so much that you cease to be anything meaningful. But in our opinion, it should be the lens through which you look at your reason for being."

They went to Prudential's chairman and CEO, Art Ryan, with their findings. He told them that unless they had a compelling business case for outsourcing, they should look for other ways to achieve their objectives. He was, however, intrigued by the possibility of outsourcing. The HR department's proposal coincided with the company's pending IPO, which occurred in December 2001. One of the companywide objectives was to reduce costs and focus on its core business in order to increase top-line revenue growth. That is what the analysts were looking for, so the timing was perfect. Ryan encouraged Darling and her colleagues to go forward and test the business case by vetting it with key individuals in each business unit.

Honing In on a Provider

Prudential is different from a lot of other companies that have and are pursuing BPO deals because in Prudential's case, the initiative began within the HR department. As we said earlier, HR executives are often too busy managing day-to-day administrative tasks as well as a variety of one-off vendor relationships to be able to step back and thoroughly examine the pros and cons of a full-scale BPO arrangement. We have also noted that many HR executives are wary of letting go of so much of the work that has been their livelihood. But at the top of the Prudential HR organization, the opposite was true. Darling, Taylor, Ramaswamy, and their manager colleagues in HR were aligned in their thinking, committed to the idea of transforming their function, and enthused about what HR could do in a transformed operation.

"We were ahead of the curve in terms of thinking about what HR's core activities could be and in terms of what could be done about the noncore activities. The more I talked to people outside, the more I realized that fact," says Ramaswamy. "Sometimes the initiative starts with the CEO. Sometimes it's the CFO or the COO leading the drive. It was rather unique that here: the HR heads were sponsoring it."

The fact that the idea stemmed from the HR department gave Taylor, Ramaswamy, and their colleagues a degree of flexibility with regard to the pace and phasing of the transformation that they might not have enjoyed had the project been foisted on them by another department. "This was not a directive from on high," Taylor reports.

"We weren't forced into it by any means. And what that meant was that we could own the project and set the pace of change with Exult."

Taylor, Ramaswamy, and others met with the business partners (vendors and service providers, both internal and external) that Prudential already had, including the company's vice chairmen, who were responsible for running Prudential's various businesses, and the HR heads of those businesses. During these meetings, they explained what they wanted to do and why. The partners were skeptical and a bit threatened. They requested regular updates and also wanted the opportunity to participate.

As part of building the business case for their plan, they solicited feedback from a wide range of individuals, including experts within the company in each of the areas where the impact of the change was going to be most acute. In fact, each of the functional owners for the areas under consideration, along with the various project teams, were asked to participate in the evaluation and answer the question, "Why not?"

"Asking 'why not' versus 'why' was critical," notes Ramaswamy, "because it helped people work through any barriers they perceived might get in the way of this effort." He cites the company's staffing organization, known as the talent acquisition group, as an example. According to Ramaswamy, leaders within the department were initially resistant. They felt that staffing was a highly strategic function that had to be done in a face-to-face environment. In addition, they believed that recruiters had to come from within the organization so that they would have firsthand knowledge of the company's culture and values system.

After repeated discussions and many iterations of "why not," the team's thinking turned around. They acknowledged that some of the company's more senior positions were already being handled by outside search firms, so using an outsourcer for all recruitment would not be that different. "At the end of the day," says Ramaswamy, "the group's leadership team realized it would still have primary accountability for company strategy and policies with respect to staffing and that they could operate more efficiently and truly realize a variable cost model by outsourcing some of their tactical functions."

Having gone through the "why not" process with a multitude of stakeholders, the HR group was ready to put together a business case for the HR policy committee at Prudential—the direct reports of chairman and CEO Art Ryan. Walking that committee through the general plan was a critical step in the process, Taylor explains, because it proved to everyone that the idea was sound, that they had thoroughly researched the implications of the change, and that the economics were compelling.

"We believed that the company as a whole was about to reorganize," Taylor says. "There was a great deal of change being proposed even as we were considering our initiative. So we did think about waiting. But then we decided to just go with it, on the theory that with change being contemplated all around, the timing was right to introduce a new cost-structure model and also to reinvent the culture of HR in tandem with the evolving culture of the company. We could wait, join, or lead. We chose to lead."

Introducing change in the midst of greater change can be a dangerous move. Sometimes when employees are faced with a great deal of instability at once, they resist change. At Prudential, because the champions of the initiative were in HR, the change-within-change idea proved to be acceptable. Although the HR staff were concerned, they worked hard to make the effort succeed. A robust communications campaign that was built on the philosophy of communicating early, often, and honestly was key to gaining support in HR. The company at large was also supportive. They saw the HR department as being at the cutting edge rather than being a stagnant reminder of the way things used to be.

Exult's Value Proposition

Prudential's HR executives were keen to identify a comprehensive, end-to-end provider. "We placed a lot of value on being able to have and manage a single relationship, as opposed to managing many separate vendors," Taylor says. Their search, begun at the start of 2001, rapidly narrowed to a few players in the emerging HR BPO vendor market.

Of the existing HR BPOs, one was in the process of being sold, which made it a less desirable candidate, and several others proved not to be able to shoulder the full responsibility of end-to-end service delivery. Michele Darling, Paul Evans, and Sekhar Ramaswamy contacted Exult in February 2001 and first met with the Exult team in April. Three months later, in July, the two companies signed a letter of intent that the two organizations would work together to conduct due diligence for about four months in order to develop a value proposition for both firms. If there was not a proposition agreeable to both parties at the end of that time, the letter went on to say, the companies could shake hands and walk away.

For Prudential, it was an attractive deal. Even if Exult did not turn out to be the right partner, the company would still have conducted a valuable review of its cost and performance structure that would support future changes. There was no fee associated with this exploration; both companies agreed to cover their costs. If, however, Prudential ultimately decided not to proceed with Exult, the company would have to pay a fee in exchange for receiving the detailed outputs created jointly by Prudential and Exult during the due diligence process.

As it turned out, the very way in which Exult and Prudential worked together during this process proved to be a positive indicator for a potential long-term relationship. Prudential, having vetted the concept of outsourcing so thoroughly, brought not only senior managers into the process but also midlevel managers and staff who had a solid understanding of how the work was being performed, what issues might arise as a result, and what a realistic transition timetable might look like. In addition, Prudential's finance department conducted a review of Exult's financial health, which culminated in an on-site meeting with Exult's CFO that focused on Exult's balance sheet and cash flow burn.

Exult matched Prudential person-to-person, function-to-function, so that there was a lead person from each company jointly responsible for the findings. For example, Ramaswamy was responsible for the teams from the Prudential side; Jay Ackerman was his partner from the Exult side. As Ackerman explains, "The goal during due diligence was to assess whether there was an operational, financial, and cultural fit between the two organizations."

"Doing the analysis together was enlightening and valuable," Ramaswamy stresses. "It was almost like a change management tool unto itself. And it gave us a free look, if you will, into how it would be to work with Exult. As it turned out, there was a very strong cultural fit."

It may seem odd to find a good cultural fit between a 127-year-old insurance and financial services company with thousands of employees and a 3-year-old firm with only 1,200 people at that time, but it was there. "Exult didn't have all these organization charts that many of our people were accustomed to, for one thing," Ramaswamy says. "The company had a dot-com feel as well. But the fit was there. Our respective leadership teams were incredibly aligned, and we all saw it during that due diligence process." For example, the work styles of the two leadership groups were similar; there was a common emphasis on using fact rather than theory as a foundation for discussions. When someone raised a question or pointed to a potential problem, the team was disciplined about turning first to available data, or setting out to gather the relevant data, rather than yielding to the temptation to talk the issue through without the benefit of good information.

There was also a common drive to ensure that the kinds of invisible protocols that block communication in so many organizations didn't get in the way. If a member of the Exult team had a question for a member of the Prudential team, or vice versa, the question didn't get lost in channels. In other words, people on both sides trusted each other enough to be up front and direct with their questions and concerns, an approach that proved valuable to both sides. Managers from Exult and Prudential alike have told us that they feel it's necessary for any firm to be as transparent as possible—with people, personalities, and information—early in negotiations in order to ensure a successful partnership down the road.

Ultimately, the due diligence effort led to a value proposition that was attractive to both parties. As Ackerman puts it, "By working side by side, we really came to understand what was critical to Prudential—immediate and ongoing cost reduction, technology enhancement, and perhaps most important, a shift to a variable-cost HR model that would support changes in company size brought on by Prudential's pending IPO." Exult committed to:

- Reducing Prudential's costs by over 20 percent.
- Maintaining service levels. For example, payroll accuracy was guaranteed at 98 percent and timeliness at 99.8 percent.
- Implementing a new leading-edge applicant tracking system that would integrate with PeopleSoft, Prudential's core HRIS system, allowing Prudential to retire an application that no longer met its business needs.
- Operating with a variable-cost structure that gave Prudential clear visibility as to how its overall cost would increase should the number of head count expand or, conversely, clarified how its overall cost would be reduced if the business contracted.

The contract was a fifty-five-page document with twenty-six attachments, including more than eleven pages of guarantees regarding Exult's performance across the key areas that Exult was taking control of.

As with other clients, Exult guaranteed to meet or improve service levels. Prudential's base metrics were quite robust, and performance was generally good to excellent. Exult and Prudential worked closely together to further define metrics that enabled both companies to understand performance and manage the relationship. The Prudential contract with Exult, unlike the BP contract, did not involve an equity purchase in the BPO provider.

The Changeover Process

The contract was signed on January 11, 2002, and announced companywide at Prudential on internal satellite TV on January 16.

The goal was to begin transferring work to Exult in mid-June and have every HR administrative process in Exult's hands by October 1, 2002.

And here's a sentence rarely seen in large-scale change efforts: the changeover process went off without a major hitch, and the schedule stuck. Although there were issues to manage, the problems did not escalate into insurmountable crises. For example, payroll, benefits, and call center support were slated to be transferred to Exult in late August. This transition required shutting down Prudential's existing benefits administration system, establishing and launching a new system with Exult partner Towers Perrin, and migrating data from one system to another. The transition affected payroll, benefits, and call center support for more than 120 employees based in Minneapolis, Minnesota, and Woodbridge, New Jersey.

Late-stage issues arose that resulted in a series of conference calls on an August weekend during which Taylor, Ramaswamy, and Ackerman jointly declared a two-week delay to allow for further testing and data clean-up. Since both organizations were clear on what risks they were willing to accept, they were able to make the decision quickly and move on to the task at hand, completing the transition. As Taylor recalls, "We had people lined up to declare Armageddon the weekend before our first payroll was going to be done. But there was also confidence on both sides. Lo and behold, when we pressed the button, our people got paid."

The payroll, benefits, and call center transitions were the most difficult: the underlying technology demanded that both processes and the call center "go live" at Exult on the same day; moreover, the new benefits solution required approximately 469,000 records to be converted from the old system to the new system. And this was all happening less than one month before the scheduled start of Prudential's annual benefits enrollment period, so any delay would have significant domino effects. Nevertheless, the transition occurred smoothly with no unforeseen issues. Table 9.1 shows the transition schedule. Payroll actually began with Exult two weeks after the original target date.

Table 9.1   Prudential's Transition Chronology

Process	Transition Date
Accounts payable	June 3, 2002
Learning and training administration	June 3, 2002
Recruiting and staffing	August 1, 2002
Benefits	September 9, 2002
Call center	September 9, 2002
Payroll	September 9, 2002
Employee data and records management	September 9, 2002
Severance and separation benefits	September 9, 2002
Compensation	September 30, 2002

Exult and Prudential had drafted a preliminary transition schedule during due diligence based on a strategy of staggered transitions to mitigate risk. The idea was to plan early movement of distinct processes where quick wins could be realized, and slower transitions in areas where new systems were being introduced, such as benefits and staffing. The company was able to support the schedule and, in fact, it moved learning and recruiting forward on the original time line. IT application support and development related to each process moved at the same time as the process.

It is also worth noting that shifting accounts payable called for two transitions because one of Prudential's subsidiaries, Prudential Securities (now part of Wachovia), had its own process. Yet that transition went through ahead of time, moving from a planned July 1, 2002, start date up to June 3. Exult and Prudential managers credit that accomplishment to an extensive amount of knowledge sharing between Exult operational staff and Prudential operational staff prior to the transition.

The Working Relationship

The Exult-Prudential relationship is, by all accounts, a trusting one. As Ramaswamy says, "We very much view them as an extension of us. We will have meetings with our senior management team in HR, and we'll include the Exult account representative. We won't have these closed-door meetings and then go talk with the vendor."

As an example of that candor, which Ramaswamy cites as a critical reason for the ongoing success of the partnership, he points to Prudential's governance structure. Prudential has a senior body, the HR policy committee, that reports directly to the chairman on issues that have HR implications, such as benefit rate changes. Ramaswamy attends those meetings, as does his counterpart at Exult, when outsourcing-related issues are discussion items on the agenda. In that way, issues that are important to Prudential are immediately brought to Exult's attention as well. Expectations are set jointly, and no one has a chance to stew over anything in private, much less let a brewing conflict fester.

Since Exult signed on, Prudential has formed a similar committee that meets monthly to talk about technology planning and evolution issues that affect HR and the company at large, including the relationships Exult and Prudential have with various vendors, performance issues, and the status of state-of-the-art software. Exult representatives, including Ackerman and others, attend those meetings. A steering committee made up of leaders from both companies also meets on a quarterly basis to assess performance, discuss issues, and consider future plans.

As Taylor puts it, "We're continually trying to marry the day-to-day management of our relationship with Exult into the fabric of the organization. We don't always agree, but because of the governance and decision-making structure we have in place, we don't have to spend a lot of time worrying about pointing fingers. And as we go forward, there are going to be opportunities for increased efficiencies. You have to have the right people at the table from both organizations in order to see those things."

Ramaswamy concurs: "Our relationship with Exult is similar in a key way to what we did before with internal services. We see Exult as part of our delivery chain, delivering services to internal customers, including employees and retirees of Prudential. We talk a lot. And we don't make a distinction that Exult is an external vendor.

Jay, Sharon, and I are always in communication. Exult is a vendor, but for this arrangement to work, they have to be at the table with us, and they are."

Results

Prudential was trying to accomplish three primary goals by contracting with Exult: cost savings, creating a variable cost HR function, and moving HR executives' focus away from detail management and toward a more strategic role:

• Cost reduction is on track with expectations. HR administrative costs overall have been reduced by more than 20 percent. Service quality has met or exceeded agreed-to levels. Accounts payable was moved to Exult on June 3, 2002, with Exult processing at 99.2 percent accuracy in the first month of operation. Payroll accuracy (using the second quarter of 2003 as a measure) is above 99.8 percent.

• The HR function has successfully become a variable-cost center, and its newly found flexibility has proven valuable. Between the time Exult began its work and early 2004, the Prudential organization changed size and scope as a result of five acquisitions and two divestitures. The HR function was able to keep pace with the resulting change in the size of the company. As Ackerman says, "Together we are able to move very quickly to understand what the financial structure in HR is going to look like if, for example, Prudential adds ten thousand people. Our structure makes the financials very transparent, and that gives Prudential HR an advantage as they consider the implications of an acquisition."

Prudential's HR managers have not completely divested themselves of administrative paperwork, but they are making slow progress in the right direction. "I would say they haven't focused on ramping up strategically as much as they thought they would, in large part due to the nature of their business," Ackerman says. Short-term savings are currently an imperative because of the economy, and so that's where the focus is. The managers are optimistic about increasing their ability to contribute to Prudential in a more strategic way over the long term.

- Prudential has not significantly increased its HR self-service platform, in part because it had a robust one before the Exult contract. Nevertheless, there is room to do more with resultant cost reductions and reductions in paperwork.

Key Learnings

There has been a learning curve. Prudential's HR executives agree that they have learned, for example, that nothing is unimportant and that any small glitch in service delivery needs to be reported right away and investigated. They have also learned to address questions and concerns immediately, so that they do not grow into major sources of tension.

Early on, for example, Ramaswamy and Ackerman found that people on both sides of the relationship were too tentative about using the agreed-on escalation process to address and resolve conflicts. As a result, disagreements and questions that should have been addressed were left for too long, eventually causing the perception that a problem was bigger than it actually was. In one case, there was a difference of opinion regarding readiness to move a critically important body of work. Different groups had used different testing methodologies, and the result was that one group felt the work was overdue to be moved, and the other group was convinced the work was not yet ready.

"It was one of those 'men are from Mars; women are from Venus' kind of things," Taylor says. "To make something like this work, you have to have a robust problem resolution and escalation process that is well articulated and understood on both sides. The parties involved should have escalated the disagreement sooner, but at the time, that wasn't clear to them." "It was a new way of working," adds Ramaswamy. "People no longer had total control of an issue, process, or decision. That's not an easy adjustment for most people to make."

To get through the transition, both teams had to draw on the strong consulting skills in their ranks to facilitate a resolution. Equally important was a renewed emphasis on turning first to the available facts, putting the data on the table, and considering the data with people from all sides of the issue present.

As Ramaswamy notes, "What it taught us was that you don't get to the eleventh hour and then debate readiness criteria. You agree on those criteria in the first hour of the process and then move forward. The goal is to seek facts and manage by them, and gather enough information to figure out what the real problem is. Symptoms (tensions, fear of retribution, fear of uncovering a larger problem or of provoking the other party) often mask the real issue. The focus needs to be on identifying and studying the facts needed to make a rational decision."

Also critical to overcoming bumps along the way was a mutual commitment to a document prepared by the transition team and released in April 2002. Among other things, this document sets out a clear outline of the individual and joint goals of both parties and also articulates the approach both organizations are expected to take. (See Exhibit 9.1.)

No doubt many organizations generate documents that on the surface look much like this one and in practice have little or no effect on how the relevant parties behave. Mission statements (and this is a form of mission statement) are often designed to be inspirational and motivational, but all too often fail because they are too vague or detached from the actual work of the organization. In this case, the partnership model is directly relevant to the relationship at hand; it reaffirms the specific tenets on which the relationship is founded and should be managed and measured. And the teams come together regularly to revisit the model and assess how they are collectively performing against its mandates.

A perennial issue for Prudential's HR senior managers is finding the right balance between hands-on involvement and an advisory role. "I get more involved in a level of detail I don't need to sometimes," Taylor says. "For example, there are times when you

Exhibit 9.1 The Prudential and Exult Partnership Model

Why Build a Partnership?

To enhance value for shareholders, customers and employees of both Prudential and Exult. In doing so, we will create a *partnership* that is *recognized internally and externally* as a model for achieving *enhanced Human Resource services* at *lower costs.*

Our Partnership Model

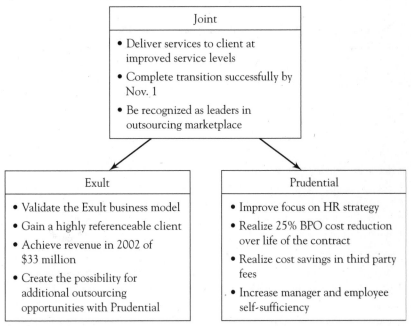

Our Goals: Outcomes We Seek to Achieve

Joint
• Deliver services to client at improved service levels
• Complete transition successfully by Nov. 1
• Be recognized as leaders in outsourcing marketplace

Exult	Prudential
• Validate the Exult business model	• Improve focus on HR strategy
• Gain a highly referenceable client	• Realize 25% BPO cost reduction over life of the contract
• Achieve revenue in 2002 of $33 million	• Realize cost savings in third party fees
• Create the possibility for additional outsourcing opportunities with Prudential	• Increase manager and employee self-sufficiency

Exhibit 9.1   The Prudential and Exult
Partnership Model, Cont'd.

Our Approach: How We Will Achieve Purpose and Goals

- *Jointly* lead and staff effort
- Manage by *fact*
- Issues will be *surfaced, defined* and *clarified* so they may be addressed quickly
- Information will be shared broadly *across* both project teams and both organizations
- We will *measure and report* our results
- *Desire to achieve mutual goals* will drive our decison making

Our Principles and Behaviors

Accountability

- We honor our commitments.
- We do what we say we will do.
- We accept responsibility for our actions.

Mutual Respect

- We honor and embrace our respective individual and corporate values.
- We believe that teammates act with good intentions for the partnership.
- We respect each other's corporate goals as defined for this partnership.
- We respect and honor the contributions made by all employees who are impacted.

Embrace Change

- We will stimulate and be open to new ideas.
- We will take calculated risks.
- We will identify and seek solutions swiftly.
- We will balance planning and action.

Teamwork

- We acknowledge that we must combine strengths and leverage talents.
- We will share backgrounds and experiences so that they can be accessed.
- We will address disagreements and conflict quickly and directly.
- We will operate as a single team and strive for "win-win" solutions.
- We will celebrate successes along the way.

Personal Growth

- We will develop strong working and personal relationships with teammates.
- We will enhance our individual skills, knowledge and abilities as part of this team.
- We will be proud of our association with this groundbreaking partnership.
- We will have fun along the way.

Source: Prepared by the Transition Team, Apr. 3, 2002.

don't see movement because people are trying to solve the wrong problem. Clarifying the issue and its root cause then allows you to step back and rely on appropriate update tools to ensure things are going according to plan."

Another consistent theme is the need to be acutely aware of the emotional ties that affect decision making. In part, this issue harkens back to the mandate to seek and manage by fact. But it also highlights the need to "put yourself in the other person's shoes" when considering their point of view. As Ramaswamy notes, "We had an old model that worked very well for us; many of us helped build it. And then suddenly there we were, moving to a new model. It's only natural that we would find ourselves at points saying 'The old way worked well. Why are we going to a completely new model? Can we find a middle ground?'"

As Exult's Ackerman notes, "As Exult has worked with Prudential, we have learned that we need to remember to look at our business through their eyes as well. For example, early in 2003, we launched our Mumbai service center. We had solid plans and a large team working to bring this center on-line. But we had not considered the work that Prudential might want us to do to help them manage and sell the change internally. There was some friction, and there were some miscues. But once we took a step back to engage Prudential, the project moved quickly, and we hit our early projected milestones."

Finally, Prudential's managers agree that it is critically important not to underestimate the amount of knowledge transfer that needs to go on. Even in a system that worked as well as Prudential's did going into the Exult transition, there was a fair amount of knowledge about the Prudential model that wasn't explicit knowledge and therefore was not apparent to Exult. The easy part is learning the business-specific policies and practices. The challenge is learning how they may be applied differently depending on the business, the function, or the individual who is affected.

Ramaswamy sums up Prudential's take on BPO succinctly and in a way that other companies would do well to consider when assessing the possibility of outsourcing HR administrative work, and also when assessing a potential BPO provider:

> The work is really done on three levels. The first level is content. What is it that we're moving? The second level is process. How do we move this work? The third level, which is critically important and also the level that we're not all trained in, is human dynamics, or emotion: the ability to understand how emotion factors into the BPO process and how to anticipate and deal with that influence.
>
> You will not find people—on either the provider side or the client side—in any transformation effort of this nature who score 10 out of 10 in all three areas. The trick is pairing up the people from the BPO provider and the client company who can complement each other to deliver on all three.

Conclusion

In many ways, Prudential's decision to outsource its HR administrative tasks and accounts payable processing, its selection of Exult as a BPO partner, and the relationship and results that have ensued are representative of what most companies going forward should expect if and when they choose to transform their HR departments with the support of a BPO provider.

By the time Prudential and Exult began discussions, Exult had developed scale and know-how. It was no longer sorting out the best and most efficient ways to operate; Exult had identified a set of preferred tools, processes, partnership goals, and relationship-governance methods and were ready to move the company beyond its start-up phase. Moreover, Exult no longer needed clients in order to build delivery capability or add to its own staff. It now was looking for new customers to take advantage of existing capacity and to get the most out of the infrastructure it had already built.

Prudential's processes made a direct transition into Exult's service delivery model without any in-between steps. Payroll and benefits moved from Prudential's locations in Minnesota and New Jersey straight into Exult's facilities in Charlotte and Houston.

There was no significant change in existing policy or procedure throughout the transition. Exult took Prudential's policies and built its delivery around them. For example, Exult supported the creation of off-cycle payroll checks in a way that mirrored how Prudential had handled it. There was also no need for Exult to create any new processes as part of the work of assimilating Prudential's HR administrative tasks; that hard work had already been done.

For the first time, Exult was working under the auspices of the business model its founders had originally envisioned. It could fold Prudential's processes into its own existing operations, thus achieving further economies of scale for itself and savings for Prudential. It could also consider what Prudential was bringing to the table in terms of existing processes and confidently assess what the best mix of old and new would be for Prudential.

Another reason the Prudential-Exult case is more in line with what will occur in future BPO arrangements is that Prudential had thoroughly examined the idea of outsourcing HR administrative tasks internally before engaging in talks with Exult. Most companies today are doing that as a matter of course before they explore BPO opportunities, but as we saw with the BP case, that wasn't always so. As a result of Prudential's careful preparation, the negotiations between Exult and Prudential were straightforward; it was comparatively easy to align goals on each side and to sort out what was going to happen, why, and when.

Prudential was keenly interested in moving toward a variable-cost model and had already determined the extent to which it could do so without the help of a BPO provider. The company also had a good understanding of its own strengths and weaknesses with regard to its cost and quality levels, which would be passed along to Exult. As a result, data collection was fairly straightforward and reliable.

Finally, during the due diligence phase of exploration, both Exult and Prudential gained enough knowledge about their own operations and each other's capabilities to set realistic and explicit expectations for the deal and the transition that would immediately follow. Most companies entering into negotiations with an HR BPO provider today should expect to do the same. And since Exult didn't need to take on Prudential staff in significant numbers, that complexity was eliminated as well. Ultimately, Exult hired fifteen people from Prudential's ranks, with most coming from the company's talent acquisition and IT organizations.

Looking to the future, the Prudential case sends a positive picture with respect to what can be accomplished with HR BPO. Positive results were realized in a relatively short period of time. It is still too early to confirm that HR in Prudential has become a strategic partner and force, but it is not too early to say that significant progress has been made.

Chapter Ten

Lessons Learned

BP, Bank of America, Prudential, and International Paper were early adopters of HR BPO. Indeed, BP was the first major corporation to adopt a BPO approach to HR administration. As such, their experiences are a bit atypical of what later adopters will experience. Nonetheless, a great deal can be learned from the experiences of these four early adopter companies.

Looking at early adopters often provides particularly good insights into why certain business models and business processes develop and are established as best practices. It also highlights the challenges of implementing change and provides valuable lessons concerning how effective new programs can be and where they should be implemented. This clearly is true with respect to HR BPO. The experience at BP, for example, led to a number of lessons that influenced how Exult has dealt with later customers. Exult's model and those of other HR BPO firms have changed as a result of these cases. Finally, these cases provide an early look at the impact of HR BPO on the HR function, as well as the effectiveness of HR BPO.

Why Companies Choose HR BPO

Without question, the top reason that BP, Bank of America, Prudential, and International Paper chose HR BPO was cost. In each of these cases, the companies were offered a cost reduction that was attractive to them. It was particularly attractive because Exult guaranteed the cost reduction, and thus they had little risk with respect to realizing cost savings. If they had tried to obtain the same cost savings without using outsourcing, there is no guarantee that they could have done so. As a result of Exult's practice of guaranteeing saving, it is likely that a major reason that companies will adopt HR BPO in the future will be cost saving. It has been established as a visible and important deliverable that HR BPO firms must offer in order to be competitive.

Beyond cost savings there are a number of other reasons that these four organizations were attracted to the idea of HR BPO. One was the idea of putting HR on the Web and establishing e-based self-service processes. This was particularly important for BP because the company wanted to use the introduction of e-HR to speed up the movement of BP onto Web-based information and transaction systems, something that the CEO, Lord Browne, strongly felt the company needed to accomplish.

Better service levels were a third reason that these companies were attracted to HR BPO. They believed that Exult, because of its focus, expertise, and ability to obtain economies of scale, could improve upon the service that the companies were getting from their internal staff groups. With its commitment to developing a core competency in HR administration, Exult convincingly argued that it would make process improvements that would upgrade service quality, reduce costs, and increase speed to levels that cannot be obtained from a staff group.

A number of research studies have pointed out that HR executives are often mired in administrative details when they should be dealing with major strategic business issues.[1] Thus, the argument that turning over HR administration to an HR BPO could free up executives to spend more time on strategic issues represented a fourth reason that HR BPO appeared to be an attractive alternative for these four companies.

The ability to analyze HR data and build data warehouses in order to address key business strategy and change management issues did not seem to be an important reason to outsource HR administration. BP, Bank of America, Prudential, and International Paper seemed much more concerned with the basic nuts and bolts of delivering services, controlling costs, and reducing the administrative burden that internal HR people experience.

An additional reason that HR BPO may make sense for organizations is the support and flexibility a provider can offer when the firm is growing or scaling down in size. With HR BPO, a firm can expand or contract its workforce without having to significantly change the number of employees it has in its HR function, and it does not need to change its HR processes. Scalability did not seem to be critical to the decision to outsource in the four cases that we studied. It did turn out to be highly relevant in the case of BP, since it added Arco soon after signing with Exult. In order to add Arco, BP simply scaled up its existing contract with Exult. This allowed it to reduce the number of HR people in Arco and gain cost savings from the acquisition that would not have been possible without an easily scalable set of HR processes and practices.

When it comes to downsizing, having an HR BPO process may be particularly advantageous. As a company has fewer and fewer employees, it clearly needs fewer people in HR. Rather than facing the pain of having to eliminate staff members, a firm that has an HR BPO contract can simply tell its vendor to reduce its level of service and not have to deal with laying off or downsizing its HR function.

Selection and Start-Up

All of the organizations studied went through extensive due diligence processes before selecting Exult. This is hardly surprising given the newness of the HR BPO business and the fact that no HR BPO firm has had a track record to look at until recently. In the future, due diligence processes certainly can be and probably should be somewhat shorter, but there is still a case to be made for an extensive due diligence process in every situation where an HR BPO relationship is being established. It is clear from the cases reviewed here that there needs to be a good fit between provider and customer. A good fit is partially a matter of whether their preferred administrative practices are similar and whether the company is ready to manage a HR BPO vendor, but it is also more than that.

Organizations in an HR BPO relationship need to work together in a partnership mode. They are in a long-term, multiyear relationship that can work only if the organizations and people trust and respect each other. Some of the key culture fit issues are the value that the organizations involved place on speed and quality and how they resolve conflict.

The four cases highlight that it is particularly important for the customer organizations and the vendor to determine whether there is a good fit in terms of the ability to work together and with respect to dispute resolution and problem solving. No contract, no matter how extensive, can cover all of the contingencies that come up, so it is critical that processes be put in place that allow organizations to deal with problems and unexpected events effectively. Obviously, dealing with them is easier when two organizations share common values and common ways of operating.

Trust between the contractor and purchaser is essential since no set of rules can define the relationship. The required relationship between the parties has been called a "clan" where shared values, common beliefs, and serial equity become foundations for sustaining the contract.[2]

Finally, it is much easier to enter an HR BPO process than to exit one. Thus, anything that can be done to determine whether the match is a good one needs to be done. A three-month or longer due diligence process is still very much in order.

The cases we studied illustrate the importance of getting the start-up of the services correct. Failures early on harm the image of the provider and make it difficult for the vendor to build credibility with the employee population. A good rule of thumb is that it is better to delay handing over the processes to the vendor than to start with a system that still requires fine-tuning and debugging.

One of the interesting points illustrated by the cases concerns the length of time needed for the start-up of a HR BPO relationship. Clearly, Exult learned a great deal about starting up relationships from the result of its difficult start with BP. Its later start-ups, with International Paper, for example, were much less complex and faster. In part, this was because they involved less of a need to standardize practices and pull together previously independent companies. Still, it is clear that Exult learned a considerable amount about how to start processes and as a result was able to move much more rapidly with its later clients than its earlier ones. This makes a strong argument for the advantages of dealing with an experienced HR outsourcer. An experienced firm is likely not only to have better knowledge about how to operate certain systems, but also to have the ability to take over HR administration for a firm much more quickly than a neophyte firm would.

HR BPO Effectiveness

It is much too early to reach a definitive conclusion about the effectiveness of HR BPO. In many respects, even the most mature example that we studied, BP, is still in its infancy. In addition, we have information only from early adopters, which may not be typical of what will occur with later adopters. It is not too early, however, to declare that all four of the organizations are showing significant positive results. All remain committed to the HR BPO approach and feel moving to it was the right decision.

Impact on HR Administrative Costs

As we noted previously, the major reason companies adopt HR BPO is to save money. In all four of the organizations studied here, this, in fact, happened. This is hardly surprising since Exult guaranteed cost savings to each of the companies. Perhaps the key point is that Exult was able to deliver on those savings and at the same time become profitable itself. Thus, Exult has established that HR BPO firms can reduce the cost of HR administration and be successful as a business. The key remaining question with respect to HR BPO is how much HR BPO can reduce administrative costs.

Because of confidentiality agreements in Exult's contracts, we cannot provide data on the amount of savings that each company was guaranteed. However, we can state that it is reasonable to expect at least a 20 percent reduction in HR administrative costs as a result of HR BPO. This is typically a savings that remains in place over the life of the HR BPO relationship. It is unrealistic to expect that HR BPO firms will be able to produce additional large savings, although they may be able to deliver some additional savings over the long term as they gain scale and improve their processes.

Speed and Quality of Service

In order to assess the impact of the Exult HR BPO relationship on the four firms' HR administrative service level, we gathered data from a number of sources. We used a short questionnaire to ask HR executives in the firms to assess the quality and speed of HR services. We also asked non-HR executives to assess the services. In addition, we conducted interviews with key HR leaders in the firms and, where they were available, looked at employee surveys on the quality of service provided by Exult.

The results of this data gathering are clear-cut with respect to speed. Installing an e-HR system with an employee self-service portal clearly accelerated the HR administrative processes in all four firms. The only qualification concerns dispute resolution.

Some HR managers pointed out that with an HR BPO, it can be difficult for employees to find an HR professional to help them with a problem that they have with an HR service. In all cases, they can contact a service center, but some employees feel that is an impersonal and ineffective way to have their grievances resolved. They much preferred being able to go to a local HR representative they knew. In some cases, the local representative was able to resolve the issue quickly because he or she had the authority to make a decision or could correct a mistake that had been made.

Overall, in our survey data, the HR executives reported a significant increase in the overall effectiveness of HR services as a result of the adoption of an HR BPO system. However, when it came to the satisfaction of company employees with HR services, HR people felt there was a slight decrease in the satisfaction of employees. This perceived decrease is open to multiple interpretations.

One explanation is that the services were not as good as the personal services that previously were delivered by the company HR staff, but this explanation is not consistent with the finding that the HR services improved. Furthermore, in each case, Exult collects data from employees on the satisfaction with the HR services it delivers. These data, which focus on both individual transactions and the overall level of HR services, show relatively high employee satisfaction levels. Since there are no "before" data, it is impossible to do a comparison with the situation before outsourcing, but it is possible to state that employee dissatisfaction does not seem to be a major problem.

Some employees did react negatively to the fact that the Exult system relies on a Web-based self-service delivery approach. Although many employees are familiar with computers and prefer to go on-line in order to get information and do transactions, the Web is a foreign, infrequent, and threatening experience for some employees. It is not surprising that individuals who are not comfortable with computer-based services would be unhappy with moving to an HR BPO that relies heavily on computer-based self-service to deliver HR administrative services. No matter how good the system is, some people will not be comfortable with it and will prefer to talk face-to-face with an individual. Thus, it is unrealistic to expect that all or almost all employees will be satisfied with the move from a traditional person-based HR administrative system to a Web-based one. All that an organization can do is make an effort to educate its employees, create a user-friendly environment, and provide support to those for whom the e-HR system is unfamiliar and unfriendly territory.

Another possible explanation is that the HR managers were a bit hesitant to admit that the services that they used to give were in fact less satisfying to employees than the ones provided by their new vendor. HR staff members and the employees they serve can develop a codependency relationship when it comes to HR administration and problem resolution. That is, they learn to depend on each other, and although the relationship may not be very efficient and may be quite costly, both become attached to it. It provides the HR staff members with a reason for being and a great deal of satisfaction when they are able to solve a problem or resolve a dispute. It allows employees to talk to a person who knows them and who they believe cares about their problem. In the case of line managers, it often allows them to hand off work that they do not particularly want to do to an HR administrator who will solve the problem. Moving to a self-service environment takes away what may be a valued, if not efficient, resource for managers.

It is too early to reach a final conclusion about how HR BPO relationships affect the quality of HR services. Clearly, HR BPO firms are on a learning curve when it comes to delivering these services and in terms of how to establish employee expectations concerning the services provided by an HR BPO. Undoubtedly adjustments will be made by providers and clients as they become more experienced in dealing with and managing an HR BPO relationship. These may include changes in the balance between the services offered by the company staff and those offered by HR BPO firms. What we can state with confidence is that in these four cases. we do not see any evidence of a major problem.

HR as a Strategic Partner

In both the interviews and the survey data, HR executives reported that moving to an HR BPO system helped them become more of a strategic partner. They suggested that it freed up their time so that they would have more time to spend on issues such as organizational change, business strategy, talent development, and advising and consulting with line managers.

Table 10.1 presents some interesting data from our survey on how HR managers in BP, Bank of America, Prudential, and Inter-

Table 10.1 Percentage of Time Spent on Various Human Resource Roles

	National Sample	Before Exult	After Exult
Maintaining records (collect, track, and maintain data on employees)	14.9	14.2	6.7
Auditing and controlling (ensure compliance to internal operations, regulations, and legal and union requirements)	11.4	11.8	9.6
HR service provider (assist with implementation and administration of HR practices)	31.3	29.0	25.0
Development of HR systems and practices (develop new HR systems and practices)	19.3	16.5	18.6
Strategic business partner (member of the management team; involved with strategic HR planning, organizational design, and strategic change)	23.2	27.5	39.1

Note: Figures are means.

national Paper think their outsourcing contracts affected how they spend their time. The table, which compares time spent by the HR function before the Exult contract and current time spent, shows a significant increase in the degree to which managers see time being spent on strategic business partnering.

Table 10.1 also shows a comparison between how time is spent in these four companies and how time is spent in a national sample of companies surveyed in 2001.[3] It shows almost identical data for these companies and for the four companies studied before they began HR BPO. But after the Exult contract, they report much more time spent on strategic partnering than in the national sample.

Table 10.2 contains additional data about HR as a strategic business partner before and after outsourcing. It shows a significant

Table 10.2 Role of Human Resources in Strategy

	National Sample	Before Exult	After Exult
No role	3.4%	9.1%	0%
Implementation role	11.6	18.2	18.2
Input role	43.8	36.4	36.4
Full partner	41.1	36.4	45.5

Note: Figures are means.

increase in the degree to which HR is a full business partner in developing business strategy from the time before outsourcing and the time after outsourcing. In the case of the national survey data, which are also presented in the table, the after-outsourcing number is higher but not significantly higher.

Overall, the data suggest that outsourcing is a way to free up HR time so that HR managers and professionals can spend more time as strategic partners. It also suggests that when the time is freed up, HR managers do play a more significant role in business strategy development and implementation.

In order to determine whether the increased role of HR executives in strategic planning is due to reduced administrative workload or new types of information and insights that are available to them as a result of having an e-HR system, our survey asked several questions about the use of HR data. HR executives were asked whether the movement to an e-HR system allowed them to do more analytics concerning the impact of HR on the business, as well as whether it provided them with new strategic direction information. The answers to these questions suggested that it did provide an increment in these areas.

HR executives said that to "some extent," it provided new strategic information and enabled the analysis of HR's impact on the business. But this was not seen as a major outcome of having an e-HR system. This is hardly surprising since most of the systems are new, and using the data from them for strategic analysis is clearly not a simple activity. Indeed, there is quite a learning curve that organizations need to experience in order for them to effectively mine the data in an e-HR system. A key issue for the future is how much of this is done. If it is done, it has the potential to make e-HR systems much more valuable and to position HR functions as a much more significant strategic partner.

Impact on HR Employees

Our cases clearly illustrate that moving to an HR BPO model reduces the number of employees that organizations need in the HR function. It especially reduces the need for call center employees and clerical employees. In some cases, it reduces the need for employees who work on employee problems and dispute resolution since these issues are typically handled by HR BPO call center employees. In the case of BP and Bank of America, some employees who were displaced by the BPO move found jobs with Exult.

Initially, many of the employees who were transferred to Exult from BP and Bank of America were upset and disappointed. They had spent their careers working for leading employers and were not happy to be relegated to working for an unknown HR start-up. Nevertheless, many of the employees who moved from BP and Bank of America to Exult now report that working for Exult is an improvement over working for the HR function of a large corporation. Partly, this seems to be a size effect. With Exult, they find themselves part of a smaller organization that is able to focus more on them, and perhaps more important, they are in a business in which they are the key to success. In an HR BPO firm, HR is the business of the firm, and as a result the employees represent the core competency of the organization. They often are in contact with the CEO and the other leaders of the organization, and they are the key human capital of the business. Thus, there is every reason to believe that working for a well-managed HR BPO firm can be more involving and more exciting than working in the staff function of a large corporation.

Not all employees who are displaced by HR BPO contracts will find jobs in an HR BPO firm. Indeed, Exult moved from taking on a significant number of employees from its original customers to ending this practice. This is hardly surprising. Once Exult staffed up, its business model called for it to leverage existing employees over a larger and larger customer base. This is a key element in Exult's business model and is necessary in order for it to offer the kind of cost savings that companies look for when they sign up with an HR BPO firm. Overall, therefore, it is reasonable to expect that the HR BPO process will lead to fewer and fewer jobs in HR administration.

One additional point is relevant here. Even if firms do not outsource HR administration, moving HR administration onto a self-service Web system will reduce the number of HR administrative employees. At this point, it is not clear whether moving to an HR BPO firm will cause larger reductions than simply putting HR administration on a company e-HR system. A guess, however, is that it will. HR BPO firms have the advantage of scale and, potentially, the development of greater expertise that may lead to their being able to operate a leaner operation with less overhead per employee served. As a result, they may end up producing the greatest reduction in the number of HR administrative jobs.

Ultimately, HR BPO may have a major impact on the work of HR professionals and executives. With time freed up from HR administrative issues, HR professionals will have to move from talking about being strategic to actually being strategic. This transition may be more difficult for some HR professionals who have spent their careers managing administrative systems. They now have to collaborate with managers to set and implement business strategies and build capabilities of talent, speed, collaboration, learning, accountability, and leadership into their organization. The skills needed to build these capabilities are different from the skills needed to do administrative HR. The opportunity now exists for HR professionals to be truly strategic business partners. The challenge is to acquire or develop the needed skills to do it.

HR Metrics Development

In all four cases, there was an improvement in the metrics used to measure the delivery of HR services. This turned out to be an important result because it allowed for significant improvements to be made.

It is worth noting that early adopter companies did not have the kinds of measurement systems in place to compare service levels (in particular, service quality) "apples to apples" before and after HR BPO. Companies considering HR BPO should utilize a period to establish a baseline against which they can negotiate a contract and ultimately measure progress. It is also worth noting, as we saw in the cases, that Exult's own measurement systems are being tuned to ensure that the outcomes being measured are relevant.

Summary of Benefits

We can now summarize the value proposition for HR BPO. Firms that choose HR BPO should expect to receive:

- Reduced administrative costs of at least 20 percent and possibly more
- Increased e-HR and employee self-service because HR administration is on-line
- Faster HR administration
- Increased quality of service to employees
- Freed-up HR leadership time from administration to use on strategic issues
- Scalability, or the ability to expand or reduce HR administrative systems as required by firm strategy
- Better HR administrative metrics

Companies considering HR BPO would do well to vet these value drivers thoroughly with HR BPO provider candidates.

HR BPO as a Business

The success that Exult has experienced with its four initial major customers has gone a long way toward establishing that HR BPO is a viable business. It has also established some of the key features of that business. First and foremost, it is a scale business that becomes more and more profitable as it achieves greater size.

Early on, Exult needed to take on the employees from its first few customers, as well as use some of their call centers and other facilities in order to service customers. It now is established to the point where it has the infrastructure necessary to service more and more employees without making proportionately greater investments in physical facilities and employees. Its capacity will be even greater after the merger because Hewitt has a substantial outsourcing capability.

The contracts that Exult has signed also clearly establish that it is a business that can involve substantial amounts of revenue. A large company that outsources HR administration can bring in $100 million or more of annual business to an outsourcing firm.

HR administration is clearly a volume business, but it is also a business that requires vendors with competency in HR processes and information technology. An important key to being successful as an HR BPO is moving toward relatively standardized HR processes that are state-of-the-art. Thus, HR BPO providers need to develop core competencies and excellent administrative practices in areas such as benefits, selection, recruiting, compensation, payroll, and a host of other HR administrative tasks. Outsourcers that do the best job of developing core competencies in these areas clearly have a competitive advantage when it comes to gaining business and being profitable.

HR BPO organizations do not just need a core competency in HR administration; they need a core competency in Web-enabled HR administration. Creating e-HR systems that offer self-service is the key to reducing the administrative costs of HR and satisfying customers. Developing sophisticated, user-friendly, Web-based administrative systems is a complex task that is time-consuming and expensive. This is one of the critical reasons why HR administration is a scale business. Once an effective software program has been developed, it can be scaled up to include hundreds of thousands, and even millions, of employees at smaller and smaller additional costs.

Exult recognizes it is in a volume business and as a result is committed to standardizing the administrative processes it provides to its customers and to moving them as quickly as possible onto the Web. This requires a good technology platform and expertise in designing, or at least identifying, the best Web-based technology that is available.

There are multiple ways to develop technology systems. HR BPOs can obtain the applications they require by buying them from one or more vendors. They can acquire them all from a single provider such as PeopleSoft, or they can buy best-in-breed applications from the many vendors that provide point solutions for particular HR processes. The key to success for an HR BPO is to differentiate itself by offering more than organizations can afford to have on their own and by creating an integrated, best-in-class technology platform. This clearly requires a well-developed core competency in HR technology and software. If an HR BPO can satisfy a diverse customer base with the same technology, it gains even further economies of scale and is likely to be more profitable.

HR BPO firms can also develop their own proprietary software. Exult has developed an employee portal as well as some of its own applications. However, it has increasingly relied on best-of-breed vendors to provide the software it needs. This is likely to be even more true in the future because HR BPO firms are unlikely to be able to afford to develop the best applications for all HR processes. Even with a growing customer base, an HR BPO firm is unlikely to have the same scale as a leading firm that sells just software. Offering a choice of applications also allows firms to customize their e-HR systems so that they fit their HR strategy.

The economy-of-scale argument clearly is key to the success of HR BPOs. Indeed, an argument can be made that leading firms will increasingly gain competitive advantage because as they add more and more customers, they will be able to hire the top HR experts, commit more and more dollars to R&D, and integrate the best technology platforms so that they will be increasingly favorably positioned in the market. In short, success in this business seems likely to lead to more success because of the leverage that scale provides.

Notes

1. Lawler, E., and Mohrman, S. (2003). *Creating a Strategic Human Resources Organization: An Assessment of Trends and New Directions*. Palo Alto, Calif.: Stanford University Press.
2. Ouchi, W. G. (1980). Markets, bureaucracies, and clans. *Administrative Science Quarterly*, 25:129–141.
3. Lawler and Mohrman. (2003).

Chapter Eleven

Outsourcing and
the Future of HR

The case studies looked at four of the early adopters of HR BPO. Recently, a number of other organizations, including Bank of Montreal, IBM, and Procter & Gamble, decided to adopt HR BPO. It now seems clear that we are in phase two of HR BPO activity. Adoption of HR BPO has moved from early adopters to progressive companies that are willing to take some risks but were not comfortable moving into an area that was new and unproven.

The number of providers of HR BPO has also increased dramatically and includes IBM, Fidelity, Hewitt, Mellon, ACS, and a number of others. Companies now have a choice of many more vendors than were available when BP made the groundbreaking decision to sign an HR BPO contract with Exult. There is every reason to believe that the increase in the number of providers will be matched by a rapid growth in the number of progressive companies that choose to do HR BPO. It is also inevitable that the demands with respect to the kinds of services they get from an HR BPO will increase, as will the services themselves. Competitiveness has a way of leading providers to improve their products.

Impact of e-HR

The movement of HR administration onto the Web is accelerating and is inevitable.[1] It is an important feature of all HR BPO contracts. The transition of HR to self-service Web-based systems is clearly not easy, nor is it something that is ever complete. Advances in software, business strategy changes, environmental changes, and changes in HR theory and practice mean that companies' Web-based systems will be candidates for change; indeed, change is necessary in order for an organization to maintain competitive costs and service levels and support its business model.

Traditional face-to-face and paper-based delivery of HR services clearly cannot compete with Web-based e-HR approaches. They are simply too expensive and slow. HR administration has to go on the Web and move into the self-service mode. Each organization needs to decide what the best way is for it to get on the Web; several alternatives are available.

Organizations can develop and operate their own software and their own systems. We mentioned earlier that Cisco, HP, IBM, and other companies did this early on and enjoyed some success. We are convinced, however, that this approach no longer makes sense. It is too expensive and fails to capitalize on the advantages size gives when it comes to developing software, new practices, and operating information systems. Thus, it is not surprising that organizations including Procter & Gamble and IBM, which developed their own customized systems, have chosen to turn over their operation and further development to HR BPO vendors. They recognize that the continued operation and development costs associated with these systems are too high for a single corporation to support and that HR administration is not one of their core competencies.

An alternative to developing company-specific e-enabled HR systems is for companies to buy and operate systems provided by software vendors. These systems can be hosted by a vendor or run by the IT department of the company. Currently, this is the approach to e-HR that is used most frequently by large corporations.[2] The two most prominent ERP companies, SAP and PeopleSoft, provide extensive e-HR software. There are also a variety of software point solutions available that organizations can buy and combine into an overall e-HR system. Using the latter approach, companies have the potential to develop a portfolio of the best HR software applications for each of their HR processes.

The choice between whether an organization adopts an HR BPO approach to developing and operating its e-HR system or decides to develop and operate its own e-HR system is a critical one. These are the two options that most organizations should and most likely will choose between. The two approaches offer different advantages and risks and place very different demands on the organization.

In-House HR Administration

There will be firms that decide, for a variety of reasons, to keep most or all HR administration in-house. So far, the ones that have made this decision seem to adopt a front-back organization structure. As noted earlier, they develop a corporate service center that deals with HR administration. It usually has a call center and a center that provides e-HR services. These centers typically buy software from one or more vendors and develop their own e-HR systems. They often outsource one or more HR processes, such as benefits administration or payroll, to a vendor or vendors.

The advantages of providing most HR processes in-house include the kind of control that comes only by directly providing the service and the opportunity to be directly aware of any problems that develop in the HR systems or, indeed, in other areas of the organization's operations. It may also lend itself to more custom solutions and approaches to HR administration. This potentially can provide a competitive advantage, although there is a question as to whether HR administration solutions can ever provide a true competitive advantage. Most likely, HR administration can only cause a competitive disadvantage when it is done so poorly that it irritates people or leads to major mistakes in employee treatment.

Whether providing HR administration in-house can reach the level of cost savings that can be reached by outsourcing is questionable. True, there is no profit margin that needs to be earned by an internal service group, but the savings, even in large firms, are limited by scale. Even the very largest firms will likely end up having only a fraction of the total number of employees that the large

HR BPO firms will have. In addition, it is unknown how effective firms that provide HR in-house will be in developing process knowledge and integrated practices that end up being better than what they might get from an HR BPO provider. To the extent that they can do this, they might be able to match the kind of cost savings that are delivered by an HR BPO firm and have better service delivery.

It is beyond this discussion to go into all the details of what it takes to operate an in-house e-HR system successfully. Needless to say, it certainly takes considerable expertise in both IT and HR process development even if some of the processes are hosted by vendors. It particularly takes a considerable amount of expertise in knowing which software is most appropriate, and how and when the software needs to be upgraded.

Although moving to an e-HR system will undoubtedly reduce the head count in HR, doing so still leaves a considerable amount of the management of the HR administration inside the organization. This means the function has to spend time managing HR administration and needs to have individuals who are skilled at running service delivery units. If some processes are outsourced, HR needs expertise in managing vendors and ways to coordinate the efforts of vendors and in-house providers. If many vendors are used, the coordination costs among vendors and melding their different services can also be expensive and time-consuming.

Outsourcing HR Administration

HR BPO firms potentially can develop a value proposition that is superior to the one that internal providers of HR services can offer. Although keeping HR administration in-house eliminates the need to pay for the overhead and profit of an HR BPO firm, it may not end up being less expensive. It sacrifices the economies of scale that are available with an HR BPO firm and generates its own overhead inside the organization. Thus, it is likely that in most cases, HR BPO firms can develop economies of scale that result in cost savings beyond what a company can develop on its own. They also have a superior opportunity to develop domain expertise. They are in a position to aggregate world-class HR process experts and world-class HR software solution experts. Because HR is their core competency, they are likely to be more efficient and improve HR processes and practices at a more rapid rate than is the internal function of an organization. The success of HR BPOs with their early adopters suggests that the advantages of an HR BPO relationship are not just wishful thinking. They can, in fact, be a reality if organizations can avoid the problems that may occur with outsourcing.

Potential Outsourcing Problems

The literature on outsourcing has identified a number of key problems with outsourcing.[3] Most of this literature has looked at IT outsourcing rather than specifically at HR BPO outsourcing, but it still is informative about the potential problems that organizations should be aware of before they enter into outsourcing relationships.

Wrong Vendor. Many of the outsourcing failures by corporations can be traced to their picking the wrong vendor or vendors. Nothing is more fundamental to the success of an outsourcing effort than the fit between an organization and its vendor. The vendor needs to have the right systems and a working style that fits with the company it is serving.

In the HR space, a number of HR vendor firms have been sold or have failed, and this is likely to continue to happen as the industry matures. Vendor stability and continuity are critical to the long-term success of an HR BPO contract. Changing vendors can lead to a major disruption in the services that an organization receives, and thus a key issue in outsourcing is the financial stability and long-term future of the vendor.

Poor Contract. Developing a good contract is critical to HR BPO outsourcing. Entering into contracts that are poorly structured can quickly lead to failure. HR BPO contracts can be too favorable to one party, lack good standards and performance expectations, and be overly rigid. With advances in technology and changes in organization size and business strategy, contract flexibility is critical. In contracts as large and complicated as those in HR BPO, many issues will remain vague and depend on trust. Thus, it is particularly important that contracts be clear about expectations, roles, and dispute resolution.

Poor Change Management.   Outsourcing a major function of a corporation raises critical change management issues. The process of change is almost as critical as the change itself. Inevitably, changes create chaos that need to be managed. There typically is a substantial dislocation of people, as well as a need to develop new expertise and transfer a considerable amount of knowledge. When this is handled poorly, an outsourcing effort can produce major problems: critical expertise can be lost, poor transfer of systems and therefore poor service levels can appear, and ultimately, an organization may have to take its outsourced activities back in-house or find a new vendor in order to solve the problems.

A particularly important feature of the change process concerns how the existing employees are dealt with. Outsourcing has a major effect on the employees in HR and a significant effect on all other employees. A major communication and training effort is needed to explain what is happening and why and to familiarize employees with the new process. If staffing in HR is being reduced, a separation program is needed that includes extensive communication about what is happening and fair treatment of terminated employees.

No Exit Strategy.   Organizations that outsource can become overly dependent on the supplier.[4] That is, they can lose their internal expertise to such a degree that they have little ability to monitor the supplier, choose a new supplier, and move their activity to a new supplier. Organizations always need to keep in mind an exit strategy from their existing HR BPO vendor and maintain a sufficient level of expertise to be able to execute the separation from their existing vendor.

Preparing for Business Process Outsourcing

BPO transactions are complex, so it is important to bear in mind some key points about how they should be designed and managed.

Costs. Organizations need to know their costs before they begin serious contract talks with any BPO provider. They need to know what it costs to run each process they are considering outsourcing. It is important to consider what they could save if they rethought or restructured the processes and ran them internally. They should also be able to calculate the cost per employee for HR administration. This cost might be something like $1,500 per employee. With this baseline, they can determine savings post-outsourcing.

Service Levels. Organizations considering BPO vendors need to establish what the current service levels are in their organization. After an outsourcing effort, the service levels perceived by employees may drop for a short time because of the disruptions associated with change, but they should quickly rise and be continually monitored. If there is no baseline, service levels cannot be tracked. In order to negotiate a reasonable contract with a vendor, organizations need to know their cost, as well as the timeliness and quality of each of the HR processes that they are considering outsourcing. In the absence of data on these, it is virtually impossible to negotiate a contract with valid performance standards. For a company that does not have good historical metrics on the effectiveness of its HR organization, the due diligence process can be particularly time-consuming and difficult. As our cases illustrate, it is important to get this piece of the outsourcing relationship right, even if it means delaying the beginning of an outsourcing contract.

Due Diligence. It is important to be vigorous and rigorous about due diligence. Can the vendor deliver what it promises? Will it be around next year? In five years? Some key aspects of a due diligence process likely will get easier in the future because reference checking will be much easier, and potential vendors will be clearer and better established. This does not, however, mean that a strong assessment process is not necessary. It is. There is no substitute for doing a thorough analysis of the capabilities of all vendors, checking their references, and previewing the kind of system that an HR BPO vendor will install.

Technology. A key issue with respect to technology is whether the processes offered by a BPO vendor fit the way the organization wants to manage its people. It needs to examine whether the way a vendor proposes to handle a particular process is compatible with the way it wants to manage its human capital. If it is not, then it needs to request that a special application be developed by the vendor or perhaps not outsource the process.

The Contract. The details of a contract deserve a great deal of attention. The best contracts contain incentive clauses that encourage both parties to improve the relationship over time. In the case of HR BPO, the relationship truly needs to be a long-term partnership between the vendor and the company. Contracts also need to be balanced. That is, they need to be win-win contracts. If they favor the company that is doing the outsourcing, there is the risk that the vendor will not survive or will need to abandon the contract. If the contract is tilted too much toward the vendor, the organization can be harmed and would have been better off keeping HR administration in-house. The contract also needs to include flexibility with respect to changes in technology and future investments. A key is the upgrading of software and e-HR systems. Finally, it must contain clauses on dispute resolution. Regular meetings to talk about changes and disputes should be built into an organi-

zation's practices and can go a long way toward eliminating the like-
lihood of a failed contract.

Transfer of Services.   Organizations need to set realistic expectations for the transfer of services. An HR BPO provider will
not be able to free HR managers from administrative drudgery in-
stantly, especially if the data given to them are less than perfect.
Often, especially in larger, decentralized companies, HR data and
practices are "hand-tweaked" on a regular basis to keep things moving smoothly and take into account special circumstances. But
when a new company steps in to run a process, those details can fall
through the cracks, resulting in a strained relationship between
provider and client at a time when cooperation and understanding
on both sides in critical.

Preparing Employees.   Overprepare the HR employees who
will be directly involved. Sometimes BPO providers take on employees as part of the transaction; sometimes they are simply taking
on the work. Both situations call for best-practice change management. Keep in mind that a BPO arrangement is more invasive than
a simple one-dimensional outsourcing job. Employees may feel
threatened; they may also suspect a larger hidden agenda. Be forthcoming regarding short- and long-term plans and goals. Share far
more information than normal. Set up telephone banks to answer
questions, have question-and-answer meetings with employees, and
be available to respond to concerns and questions.

Managing the Relationship.   Treat the relationship as the partnership that it is. Neither party can succeed if the client company
withholds information or in any other way treats the BPO provider
as less than a full-fledged member of the team. The most successful
BPO arrangements to date have regular client-provider meetings
and also have designated managers on each side—at several levels—
to keep watch over the relationship. Have periodic review and

check-up meetings to monitor the evolving relationship, and assign people to this task who will stay with it for the duration to ensure continuity in the relationship.

The Transition.   Don't underestimate the time and effort it will take to make the transition to a new system, particularly if it is Web based. It may be difficult to think this far back, but try to recall how people initially approached e-mail. Some took to it immediately, some were reluctant converts, and some to this day prefer not to use it. The transition to a Web-based system can be difficult for many employees. But so can the idea that the employee is dialing into a call center with a question rather than simply calling or visiting someone in the building as he or she may have done in the past. Allow time for employees to become comfortable with the new approach. In any change of this magnitude, at least 10 to 20 percent of the people affected will be opposed. Do not overly focus on these individuals; instead, work to satisfy the larger population.

Deciding What to Outsource

It may make sense for organizations to keep certain key processes in-house and not allocate them to an HR BPO. A strong argument can be made that if an organization wants to differentiate itself in the marketplace by doing something particularly well or in a particularly different way, that process should be kept in-house. For example, executive development is a common process that does not lend itself to outsourcing to either an HR BPO or a consulting firm. Although compensation administration from a record-keeping and payroll point of view almost always belongs in the hands of an outsourcer, the structure of the plan and advice concerning decisions and reward allocation often is best kept in-house in order to gain competitive advantage.

Finally, there may be some HR services that the organization simply wants to keep to maintain a personal touch in order to distinguish it as a unique feature of its culture. For example, it may want to show its concern for employees by confirming that each employee has a chance to meet with a company counselor when it comes to decisions about the type of health care coverage to choose or how to deal with retirement issues. Doing this face-to-face rather than on-line can be a differentiator that an organization chooses to create as a way of building its brand as an employer.

The choice between having both vendors and in-house providers, and having a single vendor that provides an integrated solution is a crucial one. The piecemeal approach requires that the organization be the integrator of the different vendors, which takes time and money. The integrated solution requires a high level of trust in one vendor and a strong partnership with that vendor.

Managing HR Outsourcing

The decision to use an HR BPO firm has significant implications for the competencies needed in the HR function. It increases tremendously the need for individuals who can manage relationships with very large vendors. Although many HR organizations have experience managing vendor contracts, they are typically of a much smaller scope. Contracts for $100 million are very different from the outsourcing contracts of $200,000 or less that most HR departments are familiar with. HR BPO contracts are particularly complex because they involve issues of software and licensing rights. This strongly suggests that the HR function needs competencies in IT, law, and finance.

One approach is to draw on the resources of the other staff functions in the corporation in order to get the skills needed to manage a large vendor contract, but that may not be the best approach. A good argument can be made that it is best to create a center of excellence focused on vendor management to deal with the outsourcing contract. This center, which would report to the HR vice president, needs to include lawyers, finance and accounting experts, and software experts.

The outsourcing of transactions means that HR will need many fewer individuals who can do HR administration. But it should not lead to a significant decrease in individuals who have a high level of expertise in each of the key HR processes. All four of the cases we studied decided to keep considerable internal expertise in HR on their staff. In effect, they retained their senior HR people to do strategic analysis and HR system design. This seems like the best position for an organization to take. It enables the organization to interact with its vendors about how processes should be designed and operated, and it allows the organization to effectively assess how well its services are being delivered.

Returning to the previous discussion about the importance of organizations' creating centers of expertise in order to have a strategic HR function, nothing in the idea of outsourcing administration invalidates that argument. Organizations perhaps have an even greater need for centers of expertise in HR processes that both assess the vendor and, if needed, facilitate the replacement of the vendor with a new one.

Expertise in compensation as well as training and development are still needed. In fact, centers of excellence in these and other HR areas are needed in order to be sure that the right systems are in place and that the data from the e-HR system are being correctly analyzed and interpreted. If anything, with the move to an e-HR system, having a large number of subject matter experts to work on analysis and business strategy is more appropriate because now they have greater data resources to work with. They can use the data in the company's e-HR warehouse to develop the kind of information they need to make much better decisions and give much better advice when it comes to the HR side of business strategy and organizational development.

HR in the Future

The case for adopting the HR BPO to do HR administration is strong; it clearly is an approach all large organizations should consider. But as an approach, it is in its infancy, as are the self-service e-HR systems it uses. There are a number of issues about the development of HR BPO and HR that firms need to consider as they make decisions about how they will design and operate their HR functions.

Business Strategy

A major area where HR BPO providers need to improve in order to meet the demands being placed on the HR function is in the area of change management and business strategy. It is inevitable that they will improve their service level on basic transactions and improve the software so that self-service will be easier, more user friendly, and available to more and more of the members of organizations. In short, they are likely to improve constantly in the degree to which they meet the basic administrative service demands of an organization.

In order to meet the demands placed on HR today outsourcers need to do more than just deliver basic services, however. They need to provide data and mechanisms that will allow organizations to develop better strategies, make better business decisions, and better implement business strategies. Data from outsourcers can provide valuable insights about how strategies are working and what might be expected in different strategic scenarios. As they gain clients, they are likely to be able to provide valuable normative data as well as analytic models.

The experiences of BP, Bank of America, International Paper, and Prudential all suggest that Web-based systems can help HR become more of a strategic partner by reducing its administrative load and increasing its credibility as a result of reducing HR administrative costs. Going beyond this requires an integrated set of e-HR programs and metrics that allow for the analysis of the effectiveness of programs, the utilization of human capital, assessment of the desirability of different uses of human capital, and different approaches to obtaining it.

Metrics Development

The adoption of an HR BPO approach should lead to improved metrics about how well the HR function is operating. Indeed, this is a key feature of most HR BPO contracts and thus is an important development associated with engaging an HR BPO firm. HR BPO firms, however, need to go beyond simply having metrics showing how well HR administration is going. They need to provide metrics that allow firms to more effectively analyze and allocate their human capital. They need to include such things as competency models that identify the skills of individuals and help the organization move into new business areas.

HR systems need to be developed that provide more data on the condition of the human capital. Measures are needed of how satisfied it is, how committed it is to the organization, the rate at which it turns over, and a host of other issues that assess the readiness and the ability of the organization to perform. These data, which are already collected by the HR organization in many companies, need to become part of an integrated Web-based system and related to organizational outcomes. This is where analytics can help an organization diagnose what is and what is not working and make improvements in its practices and programs.

Expert Advice and Management Tools

Electronic HR systems can be an effective way to provide just-in-time, expert advice on how to do compensation administration, deal with problems involving difficult employees, and manage a whole host of other HR management issues. In essence, they can provide certain types of coaching and counseling. By delivering them as needed, they can speed up the work of managers, not to mention giving them the information they need in order to improve their decision making.

Once the decisions are made, a great deal of managerial time can be saved by providing e-enabled managerial tools that implement the decisions instead of more forms to fill out and long waits for reviews and approvals. Tools can be developed that automatically approve good decisions, give advice on how others can be improved, and provide data on decision-making patterns in an organization. Compensation management is one area where managerial tools already exist. The Kadiri tool, which Bank of America uses, speeds up the pay allocation process, reduces the workload of managers, and allows senior managers an overview of how pay is being managed.

Integrated Systems

HR BPO providers do not need to create their own HR applications, but they do need to be able to identify and integrate best-of-breed applications. They need to be able to identify the best compensation tools, the best performance management tools, and the best applicant management tools and put them into their portfolio of offerings. It is inevitable that with the large number of companies that are developing new software applications, no one company, even one as good as PeopleSoft or SAP, is going to have the best technology to do every HR process. In fact, there almost always will be at least one tool that is better than the tool that is provided by an ERP vendor. HR BPO firms can capitalize on this fact if they have the ability to identify and integrate multiple best-in-breed application tools. They can come up with a system that produces a total HR solution that is superior to what any ERP company can provide.

Problem Monitoring

It is critical that HR BPO firms be able to monitor the types of issues that come up in HR administration and provide information about them to their customers. With HR BPO, there is always the risk of an organization's losing touch with its workforce. When employees talk to an HR representative, the representative is likely to hear not only about the administrative issues that the employee has but also about how things are going and what is happening in the organization. In the best of all cases, HR representatives are sensitive data gatherers and pass on to the right members of the organization key insights about important changes in the organization and employee reactions to what is happening. Given this information, the organization is able to act quickly and decisively to clear up any problems in their early stages.

Outsourcing HR administration runs the risk of eliminating this channel of communication from employees to the rest of the organization. It does not have to, however. HR BPO firms certainly can collect these kinds of data and report them. But this is not likely to happen unless there is a conscious effort made on the part of the HR BPO firm to collect these data from call center employees and on-line surveys and report them on a regular basis to the management of their customer firm.

Organization Size

Organization size is a critical issue in determining the potential gains available to organizations through HR BPO. Exult and the other major HR BPO firms so far have focused their efforts on large global organizations. In many respects, large organizations are the ideal customer for the business model that Exult has developed. It is a scale model that becomes more profitable the more employees who are served. Large companies offer the opportunity to add tens of thousands, and in some cases hundreds of thousands, of new employees. Large companies also are often the easiest to deal with because they already have relatively well-developed HR practices and systems and are sophisticated customers. They are used to dealing with vendors, often know their costs, and are clear about what they want from vendors. They also are likely to have well-developed HR processes and as a result are relatively easy to convert to a self-service e-HR system.

Smaller companies—that is, those with an employment base of fewer than five thousand employees, and particularly those with an employment base of, say, fewer than two thousand—perhaps have the most to gain from adopting an HR BPO solution. They do not have enough employees to get many economy-of-scale advantages from doing HR work in-house, so they often have the most to gain from using HR BPO. They also may not have as much expertise about processes and process development as do larger firms. Thus, they get not only scale from using an HR BPO firm, but also expertise and process development that otherwise would not be available to them. Finally, they are likely to have the least expertise when it comes to integrating software solutions and developing HR metrics. To the degree that these can be provided by an HR BPO, mid- to small-sized firms have even more to gain.

The major issue with medium and smaller-sized firms is whether they can be profitably served by HR BPO firms. Since they do not have scale, HR BPO firms may not find them as attractive a customer as are larger firms. Obviously, however, there are many more of them than there are large firms, and by producing standardized HR BPO options it seems likely that HR BPO firms can develop a profitable business by serving them. Some HR BPO firms are signing up smaller firms; thus, there is good reason to believe that HR BPO firms will develop to serve the smaller company market. Indeed, they may end up being served by an entirely different set of HR BPO firms than serve the largest customers. In the case of small and medium-sized companies, the contracts are likely to be more standardized, as are the product offerings, and the e-HR systems perhaps a little less well developed. Nevertheless, the gains realized by the firms are still likely to be well worth switching to an HR BPO supplier to obtain.

International Challenges

Global companies need global HR systems. This typically means delivering HR services in multiple languages. Unfortunately, putting material in multiple languages works against the economy-of-scale argument for HR BPO since many companies do not have large numbers of people speaking languages other than English. It is possible, however, that as HR BPOs gain more clients, they will also gain large numbers of people speaking multiple languages and make it feasible for them to provide most or all of their services in multiple languages.

Data Privacy

Privacy regulations in many countries need to be dealt with in order to operate multinational e-HR systems. For example, in Europe, there are limitations on the ability to move and store employee data outside their country of origin. Ways need to be developed to protect confidentiality and at the same time allow for global HR administration and human capital management.

Conclusion

In order to deal with the kinds of deliverables that are being demanded of them, HR functions need to reinvent themselves. They need to be able to deliver administrative services effectively and increasingly offer strategic advice and services. They need to do this in a world of increasingly rapid change and the movement of most company functions onto the Web. HR functions need to join in and become part of the movement of business onto the Web. In addition to moving their administrative functions onto the Web, they need to create Web-based metric and analytic models that provide the kind of human capital information that improves the effectiveness of organizations.

Every HR function needs to figure out the best way that it can simultaneously deliver low-cost, high-quality HR transactions and operate as business and strategic partners. One viable way to accomplish this is to outsource HR to an HR BPO firm and restructure the HR organization in ways that will focus it more on vendor management and strategic business issues. It is not the only way, but it is one that deserves consideration by every organization as it explores how it can meet the increasingly competitive demands that HR functions face.

Notes

1. Ulrich, D. (2000). From e-business to e-HR. *Human Resource Planning Journal*, 23(2):21–40.
2. Lawler, E., and Mohrman, S. (2003). *Creating a Strategic Human Resources Organization: An Assessment of Trends and New Directions*. Palo Alto, Calif.: Stanford University Press.
3. Lemy, J. B. (2003). The seven deadly sins of outsourcing. *Academy of Management Executive*, 17(2):87–98.
4. This has been called "small numbers bargaining" in the economic literature: Williamson, O. E. (1979). Transaction cost economics: The governance of contractual relations. *Journal of Law and Economics*, 22:233–261. Williamson, O. E. (1975). *Markets and Hierarchies: Analysis and Antitrust Implications*. New York: Free Press.

Index